The *Evidence* of *Faith*

Timothy P. Mahoney

with Robert Noland
and Steven Law

THINKING MAN MEDIA

For further information visit:
http://www.PatternsOfEvidence.com

The Evidence of Faith, by Timothy P. Mahoney, with Robert Noland and Steven Law.

First Published in the USA in 2017 by Thinking Man Media, 6900 West Lake Street, St. Louis Park, MN 55426 . Published in association with the literary agency of WTA Services, LLC and 517 Resources, Inc., Franklin, Tennessee.

225 pages
ISBN: 978-0-9864310-4-3
© 2017 Thinking Man Media

Bolded text in Scripture passages has been added by the author to indicate emphasis.

Book Design: Kevin O'Neill, www.KevinOneill.com
Proofing: Christy Distler
Typeset in Garamond ITC Pro and Franklin ITC Pro.
Printed in USA

TABLE OF CONTENTS

BONUS VIDEOS ONLINE

featuring Kevin Sorbo and Tim Mahoney

To further enhance your understanding while reading
THE EVIDENCE OF FAITH, Thinking Man Media is
providing you with the following web link:

http://patternsofevidence.com/evidenceoffaith/

Here you will find insightful web videos including a lively
discussion with Kevin Sorbo and Tim Mahoney on the
connection between faith, reason, and evidence, the importance of a historical Bible and why asking questions is vital
for your personal and spiritual growth.

These and other resources will help you facilitate a small
group discussion.

INTRODUCTION

The Evidence of Historical Reality

When we submit our lives to what we read in scripture, we find that we are not being led to see God in our stories but our stories in God's. God is the larger context and plot in which our stories find themselves.
— *Eugene Peterson* [1]

"In the beginning, God created …"

These five words are quite possibly the most crucial in any language for it is in this phrase we have the opportunity to find:

- *What* happened
- *When* it happened
- *Where* it happened
- *Why* it happened
- *Who* made it happen

The "it" is life itself. This is, also of course, if you choose to believe the words of the Bible. If not, you certainly have a myriad of possibilities and options available. But you must eventually make a choice, even if what you choose is to not believe at all.

However, the commonality for each possible origin is that you have to take it on faith. Why? Because no one living at this time on Earth is an eyewitness who can testify to the beginning of mankind. So faith is a necessary action, even if you believe that creation was simply random. Therefore, faith is a non-negotiable to believe in any starting point of the world or any creator who lays claim to how we began.

For our purposes in these pages, we are working from the same assumption with which I began in my own life: the Bible is true, and those five words—"In the beginning, God created"—are the truth. Now, in taking this position and accepting a single-origin belief as true also equals declaring all others are not true. This then places a sense of responsibility in understanding all we can about what we believe. My own twelve-year journey toward creating the documentary film *Patterns of Evidence* took place out of this very paradigm.

Straight out of the gate, the Bible offers both the beginning of present reality and the starting line of history. We continue to live today in the same realm or reality that God created on that very first day and set into motion. This event recorded in the first verse of the first chapter of Genesis 1 is the baseline for the evidence of our world and mankind, the origin of our plumb line that runs throughout the human timeline right into the present. The end point is, quite obviously, located in the future somewhere, visible and known only to the Creator. If He determined the beginning, He also determines the end.

So, from Genesis we move on into mankind's creation and eventually into a people group, a nation to which God forever connected Himself, led by men with whom the Creator spoke and interacted.

David Rohl, Egyptologist, historian, author, and, as a result of this journey, my friend, stated, "People dismiss the Bible as a work of fiction. But what happens if it's not? What happens if it's a real history, a history of a people we call the Israelites? Then it would become the first history book in the world. It predates Herodotus by one thousand years. Herodotus is supposed to be the first historian, but in fact I think Moses is. And it spans about four thousand years of time as well."

World religions and belief systems are most often based upon:
- A person's or a group of people's developed spiritual worldview
- An ancient text written by an unknown author
- A person's proclaimed revelation
- Traditions passed down through generations
- A combination of any of the above factors

However, the Christian worldview is different because the God of the Bible can be discovered through two crucial elements. Let's look at Him through these lenses. The first is ...

History

Webster defines the word *history* as a "chronological record of significant events; a branch of knowledge that records and explains past events."[2]

As the Creator, God chose to enter mankind's realm at distinct times, creating ordained and divinely appointed moments that could be seen, heard, experienced, witnessed, and recorded. An invisible and omnipotent God could have easily made certain His presence was never traceable or documentable, but He determined to do quite the opposite so man could have the opportunity to engage and experience Him.

God chose to provide both a path ("chronological record of significant events") and patterns ("a branch of knowledge that records and explains past events") for us to follow.

And there was evening and there was morning, the first day. (Genesis 1:5)

And there was evening and there was morning, the second day. (Genesis 1:8)

First day and then the second—a path. Evening and then morning—a pattern.

As an infinite and omnipresent Being, God had no need to delineate the morning from the evening, one day from another day, but He knew we would. Therefore, He initiated a pattern of events, not a stream of consciousness—footprints traveling and traceable throughout time, not random bookmarks in the universe.

God created history especially for us, to intervene and communicate with us, by interjecting Himself into:

- **Moments in recordable chronology in the timeline of actual people**

When Abram was ninety-nine years old the Lord appeared to Abram and said to him, "I am God Almighty; walk before me, and be blameless, that I may make my covenant between me and you, and may multiply you greatly." (Genesis 17:1–2)

When did God make this statement to Abram? When Abram was ninety-nine. Did He highjack his brain? No, He appeared to him in a personal experience. A pin was dropped on the timeline of a human life to be locatable and verifiable.

Moses and Aaron did so; they did just as the Lord commanded them. Now Moses was eighty years old, and Aaron eighty-three years old, when they spoke to Pharaoh. (Exodus 7:6–7)

When did Moses and Aaron carry God's message to Pharaoh? When Moses was eighty and Aaron was eighty-three. A marker was placed in the lives of two brothers at a set time on their individual paths as well as in their relationship to one another.

- **Geographical locations**

And the Lord appeared to him by the oaks of Mamre, as he sat at the door of his tent in the heat of the day. (Genesis 18:1)

The Lord came down on Mount Sinai, to the top of the mountain. And the Lord called Moses to the top of the mountain, and Moses went up. (Exodus 19:20)

Throughout the Bible, specific locations are recorded on a regular and frequent basis. This intentional strategy connects known events to geography on a map.

- **Recorded cycles of the calendar directly connected to events**

On the third new moon after the people of Israel had gone out of the land of Egypt, on that day they came into the wilderness of Sinai. They set out from Rephidim and came into the wilderness of Sinai, and they encamped in the wilderness. There Israel encamped before the mountain, while Moses went up to God. (Exodus 19:1–3)

Seven full days passed after the Lord had struck the Nile. (Exodus 7:25)

In these and countless other examples in Scripture, the calendar was connected to an event that would be known by many. This is not unlike our language of making statements such as, "The accident happened last Friday, two days before his twentieth birthday." Events are placed into a real-time context for both immediate verification and maximum comprehension.

- **Remembrances of known experiences and evidence**

Then Joshua called the twelve men from the people of Israel, whom he had appointed, a man from each tribe. And Joshua said to them, "Pass on before the ark of the Lord your God into the midst of the Jordan, and take up each of you a stone upon his shoulder, according to the number of the tribes of the people of Israel, that this may be a sign among you. When your children ask in time to come, 'What do those stones mean to you?' then you shall tell them that the waters of the Jordan were cut off before the ark of the covenant of the Lord. When it passed over the Jordan, the waters of the Jordan were cut off. So these stones shall be to the people of Israel a memorial forever." (Joshua 4:4–7)

"Only take care, and keep your soul diligently, lest you forget the things that your eyes have seen, and lest they depart from your heart all the days of your life. Make them known to your children and your children's children." (Deuteronomy 4:9)

Memories and recollections are often cited and make regular appearances throughout Scripture. Recalling what God had done was consistently encouraged, making history a vital aspect of living and growing in a current and continually updating life of faith. Historical building blocks create a firm foundation of certainty.

These aspects of the Bible's language connected to Christianity's origins contained in Scripture are unique and differentiate this text from all other religions and belief systems throughout history. There is a direct connection to human events and consistent engagement with mankind's timeline.

The second lens through which we may view the God of the Bible is ...

Reality

As the Creator, God could have spoken straight into the mind, taking control much like Yoda as a Jedi Master or like J.A.R.V.I.S., running Iron Man's suit. Being comprised of spirit, God could have also tapped directly into and overridden man's soul. He could have made mankind like robots on an intellectual level, created only to do His bidding with no choices, thoughts, or emotions allowed. But He did none of this. As a loving Father, He brought everything to our level and understanding to provide the highest form of love and freedom.

As God desired to intervene and communicate with mankind, He used the reality He had created for us through:

- **Words spoken directly to people**

Now the Lord said to Abram, "Go from your country and your kindred and your father's house to the land that I will show you." (Genesis 12:1)

Thus the Lord used to speak to Moses face to face, as a man speaks to his friend. (Exodus 33:11)

While Scripture certainly has accounts of people hearing God's audible voice, we cannot assume every instance in the Bible was audible and not that different from our own experience of hearing Him through our own spirits connected to the Holy Spirit. Regardless of messages being public or private, God has spoken to His people individually and corporately inside our reality throughout all of history.

- **Natural elements such as fire and clouds**

And the angel of the Lord appeared to [Moses] in a flame of fire out of the midst of a bush. (Exodus 3:2)

And the Lord went before them by day in a pillar of cloud to lead them along the way, and by night in a pillar of fire to give them light, that they might travel by day and by night. (Exodus 13:21)

Having made everything in Heaven and on Earth, as well as placed all natural law into order, God may intervene and control any element for His purposes. He uses His natural creation to speak supernaturally to His created children.

- **Miracles (supernatural provision or destruction)**

Then the Lord said to Moses, "Behold, I am about to rain bread from heaven for you, and the people shall go out and gather a day's portion every day." (Exodus 16:4)

Then Moses stretched out his staff toward heaven, and the Lord sent thunder and hail, and fire ran down to the earth. And the Lord rained hail upon the land of Egypt. (Exodus 9:23)

God has and will bring the supernatural world into the natural when He desires. His works come into our physical realm to accomplish His will.

• Representatives, messengers, and mediators

God said to Moses, "I am who I am." And he said, "Say this to the people of Israel, 'I am has sent me to you.'" (Exodus 3:14)

The Lord said to Joshua, "Today I will begin to exalt you in the sight of all Israel, that they may know that, as I was with Moses, so I will be with you." (Joshua 3:7)

Generation after generation, the people who believed God and obeyed Him have been entrusted with both His words and work to be His representatives to mankind. The amazing aspect of this paradigm is that any human may choose to experience God's conversion and calling to become His ambassador. His invitation to all shows no favoritism (Romans 1:16; 2:11).

All this is from God, who through Christ reconciled us to himself and gave us the ministry of reconciliation; that is, in Christ God was reconciling the world to himself, not counting their trespasses against them, and entrusting to us the message of reconciliation. Therefore, we are ambassadors for Christ, God making his appeal through us. We implore you on behalf of Christ, be reconciled to God. For our sake he made him to be sin who knew no sin, so that in him we might become the righteousness of God. (2 Corinthians 5:18–21)

But sinful man has always questioned both reality and history, particularly where God is concerned. Therefore, the reason He told us to always remember His works is because we so easily can and do forget Him. Or maybe the more appropriate word is we ignore what we have experienced and evidenced. That is exactly what happens when both reality and history "depart from our hearts" as we read earlier in Deuteronomy 4:9. When God does not serve our purposes or do our will, we choose to forget Him and His works. This is the state of sin. This continual battle of our fallen state is exactly why God inspires us to regularly "make known what our eyes have seen."

With the Bible as its foundation, Christianity as a belief system outlines all the necessary key components for depicting God while offering a comprehensive reality and history of man, communicating:

- The origin of mankind
- The history of mankind
- The problems created by mankind
- God's consistent and direct interaction with mankind
- God's intervention to save mankind
- God's invitation for eternal life offered to mankind
- God's ongoing relationship with mankind

So a Christian—one who believes and receives these elements as truths to live by—has based personal salvation on placing faith in concepts that they have decided were, are, and will be true both in history and reality. Some of these include:

- Jesus was sent from God to save us.
- Jesus was and is a real Person.
- Everything the Bible states about Jesus is true.
- All that Jesus said and taught is true.

Doubt's Birthday

One of the perplexing questions and dilemmas for man has always been faith versus evidence. Most often these two topics are approached as opposites in that faith is truly exercised when no evidence exists, and when evidence is present, then no faith is required. But in reality, faith and evidence make great partners that take turns leading, according to the

circumstances. It is best when we arrive at a balance between these two corresponding, not opposing, forces.

But where did this battle of belief come from? What is the origin of mankind struggling with faith while demanding evidence? What has made man long for eternal life yet also be so cynical of the one faith (Christianity) and book (the Bible) that makes a direct and consistent connection from God to man? Where did this mindset begin? Let's return to the beginning ...

God made man:

Then the Lord God formed the man of dust from the ground and breathed into his nostrils the breath of life, and the man became a living creature. (Genesis 2:7)

God gave Adam a work to do and instructions for living:

The Lord God took the man and put him in the garden of Eden to work it and keep it. And the Lord God commanded the man, saying, "You may surely eat of every tree of the garden, but of the tree of the knowledge of good and evil you shall not eat, for in the day that you eat of it you shall surely die." (Genesis 2:15–17)

God made woman from man, for man:

And the rib that the Lord God had taken from the man he made into a woman and brought her to the man. (Genesis 2:22)

God made a quite intriguing decision. He allowed His defeated enemy access to the same Earth where He placed His most precious creations. This was a calculated design "to make known the riches of his glory for vessels of mercy, which he has prepared beforehand for glory"—even after Satan's exile from Heaven (Romans 9:22–24).

Now the serpent was more crafty than any other beast of the field that the Lord God had made. He said to the woman, "Did God actually say, 'You shall not eat of any tree in the garden'?" (Genesis 3:1)

By giving all His created beings the choice of free will, He made no one to be robotic and automatic in their beliefs and actions. So, the serpent, the Enemy, "the accuser of our brothers" (Revelation 12:10), uses this freedom to manipulate words and create a question. The first "Did God actually say ...?" was born here. Doubt had a birthday. And sin itself was about to be born as well, right from this very question.

God's will and desire would have been for Adam to step up, defend his bride, and overcome the Enemy, setting things right. After all, God had given Adam the instructions for the garden before Eve was even created. But the choice to obey or not obey was in place, and Adam decided not to intervene and take action. The man made his choice; therefore the woman followed and made hers when confronted. This changed everything forever.

But it did not affect a vitally important detail: God's interaction with mankind.

But the Lord God called to the man and said to him, "Where are you?" (Genesis 3:9)

God's response was not to destroy man and delete him. He went looking for the couple, and, when you view all of Scripture as a whole, He still seeks anyone who is lost to this very day. Once God began looking that fateful hour, He never stopped.

When Jesus came, He said, "For the Son of Man came to seek and to save the lost" (Luke 19:10). God began the work of redemption when Adam fell and Jesus finished that work on the cross, and now the Holy Spirit offers this to all to this very day.

But regardless of God's activity throughout history, "Did God actually say ...?" has been expanded into "Is there really a God?" and then the more personal affront of "Who could rationally believe in God at all?" These rebellious questions challenge both reality and history.

Just as believing in God requires faith amidst evidence, disbelief in Him requires both these same elements. Even the atheist and agnostic must place faith in the fact that there is nothing in which to place faith and decide their findings of evidence result in believing there is not enough evidence to believe.

In our Christian worldview, mankind, being made by God in His image (Genesis 1:26), has eternity built into its DNA. Living in a sinful state and left to his own imagination and devices, man has created many forms of religion—reaching out and seeking to find God and, of course, eternity—on his own.

Therefore, here are two crucial questions for every Christian:

1. How important is accurate biblical history to the validity of faith?
2. How important is it to faith that all the events of the Bible were reality and actually happened?

Elephants in the Room

Let's go ahead and recognize the "elephants in the room" where Christians meet to study the Bible and talk about beliefs: the questions of "What if I'm wrong?" "What if the stories of the Bible and Christianity are just myths, fables, or grand stories someone made up?" and the largest "elephant" of them all, "What if Jesus wasn't who He claimed to be?"

God asks for our faith in that which we have not personally seen with our eyes, while at the same time supplying ample evidence to show His Word is trustworthy and the Object of our faith is on a firm foundation. While many today might accuse biblical faith of being just a blind leap in the dark, God has always backed up His followers with history and reality, therefore giving assurance to belief.

Let's face it. As long as we are human, there is always some element of fear and doubt mixed in with belief and faith. Regardless of the amount of evidence before us, we can decide we have no faith in what we do see, much less what we do not see! Often the level of fear versus faith can be based on the circumstances of any given day and our response to them. Both our reality and history of God are constantly challenged by our own question of "Did God actually say …?"

Based on God's interaction with mankind since the start of Genesis 1:1, you must now bring these debates, questions, and points home to where, regardless of how you believe or where you stand on God, the Bible, or these issues, you do understand that these concepts affect you and your eternity. Inside these pages, we want to continually zoom in from the big picture right to your own mind and heart, just as my journey has led me to do in my own.

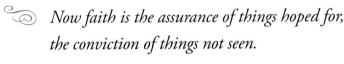 *Now faith is the assurance of things hoped for, the conviction of things not seen.*

(Hebrews 11:1)

Introduction Discussion Questions

1. Discuss the importance of each of the five words: "In the beginning, God created ..."

2. Do you agree or disagree that any origin belief requires faith, even if you choose to believe in nothing? Explain your answer.

3. Why is history important to our faith or any origin belief—both the path and the patterns from the past?

4. Discuss the four elements of history in the Bible. Which stood out to you? What did you learn?
    1. Moments in recordable chronology in the timeline of actual people
    2. Geographical locations
    3. Recorded cycles of the calendar directly connected to events
    4. Remembrances of known experiences and evidence

5. Discuss the four elements of God's intervention in reality recorded in the Bible. Which stood out to you? What did you learn?
    1. Speaking directly to people
    2. Natural elements such as fire and clouds
    3. Miracles
    4. Representatives, messengers, and mediators

6. Regarding the seven key components listed on page 13, do you feel the Bible offers substantial historical evidence for the origin of man and his history? Explain your answer.

7. Why do you think God would place His enemy in the same realm as His creation, while also allowing complete freedom of choice?

8. Discuss these two questions: How important is accurate biblical history to the validity of faith? How important is it to faith that all of the events of the Bible were reality and actually happened?

9. What do we tend to do with our "What if I'm wrong?" questions regarding God, Jesus, and the Bible? Why?

10. How might honestly and gracefully discussing our "elephants in the room" faith questions help us grow in our spiritual maturity and relationship with God?

 CHAPTER 1

The Red Sea to the Resurrection

If Jesus rose from the dead, then you have to accept all that he said;
if he didn't rise from the dead, then why worry about any of what he said?
— Tim Keller [3]

When I was eleven years old, I arrived home from playing at a friend's house to find my mom and my uncle loading the car with suitcases. In that moment, my world came crashing down. In an instant, my family was forever broken. The life we had known was suddenly, with no warning, over.

My mom, my younger brother, two younger sisters, and I were forced to escape our home in Minneapolis and go to live with relatives. This tragedy happened in the middle of the school year and was very difficult for all of us. No more family vacations, playing in the park, or fishing trips. For a number of reasons I won't go into here, the short story was that the marriage was over and my dad was gone.

Statistics alone tell me that a great number of you reading these words know this pain—this gut-punch to the heart that takes many years to overcome. These kinds of life-altering moments shake us deeply, creating long-lasting insecurity and questions.

We soon moved again to a home in another community. In a very short time, I had been in three different school systems, creating a chasm of emotional and intellectual disconnection. As I fell behind in my studies, I became insecure about my ability to learn. That lasted until the eleventh grade when my history teacher, Mr. Hall, said a very significant thing to me: "Mr. Mahoney, that was a very good answer." He made that comment in front of the entire class, which made me feel pretty good. Something I had experienced far too little of. But most importantly, at that moment a light came on in my head. Maybe, just maybe, I wasn't so stupid after all. Maybe I could learn. That was the first time in a very long time that I felt good about myself. And I wanted the feeling to last.

Over these many years of working with countless people, I have found that far too many of us, because of traumatic and hurtful pasts, feel "less than." We come to believe we are just not very smart. But I have come to the conclusion that this is simply not the case. We all have the God-given ability to think, to reason, and to solve, and, no matter our background or story, we must each awaken this great gift to explore, test, learn, and expand who we are.

Growing up in a single-parent home, my mother would read us the stories from the Bible. I could see she had a deep faith that these accounts were true and that they gave her great encouragement and hope to press on in her own life, no matter the difficulties we had as a family and what she faced. The plight of the Israelites and God's constant intervention brought my mom comfort in her own struggles. This connection between the stories of this Holy Book and my mother's faith made a profound impact on me at a young age.

So, having been raised as a Christian, I believed the stories of the Bible to be true. But as I grew older, I was challenged on many fronts to question and lose those beliefs, dealing with my own personal version of "Did God actually say …?"

But I hadn't yet encountered any real intellectual challenges to my faith. I didn't know what was coming that would shake me to the core. For the most part, I believed that there had to be evidence to support these incredible

stories, even though like many of us, I had questions. I just wanted to know the truth.

In 1985 I began making TV commercials and corporate videos. This paid the bills but didn't fully satisfy my creative interests. What I really wanted to do was make films that explored the big questions I had about the world. I guess it was only natural that I would become a documentary filmmaker, because true stories have always had much more power and influence over me than fiction.

Career, Christ & Controversy

My career path merged with my search for truth in 2002, as I began a journey to investigate the archaeology of the Bible. I was excited to start a new project that was at the core of so many of my own questions. I was to film amateur Exodus explorers in the Sinai Peninsula as they searched for the route the ancient Israelites might have taken after their Exodus from Egypt. The prospect of uncovering events from the past fascinated me.

As I interviewed professional archaeologists about this search, I was surprised when one of them said, "What's the point of looking for the route if the Israelites never existed in Egypt in the first place?" I couldn't forget that remark. It troubled me. It shook me. Like so many people, I didn't realize that the events of the Exodus were now, for the most part, dismissed by mainstream scholars. Somehow I had missed that memo at church.

Whether I liked it or not, I would have to be true to my nature and delve into this topic, searching for answers to this 3,500-year-old mystery. And there were many more conflicting comments to come.

Israeli archaeologist and author Israel Finkelstein from Tel Aviv University declared, "The Exodus did not happen in the way it is described in the text on the background of the 13th century BC."

Norma Franklin, an archaeologist from the University of Haifa, working on-site since 1992, stated, "My easy answer to you, as an archaeologist, would be to say it didn't happen. Not in the way it's written down in the Bible. In the old days, of course, most archaeologists read the Bible as a guide to the

Holy Land. We don't do that now. Everything that we know today is based on excavations, on surveys, on data. If we didn't have the Bible, we would never, as archaeologists or as Egyptologists, be able to say this happened. A mass exodus of people from one nation with a long journey of forty years? Of course, you wouldn't have forty years—I mean, forty years is more than a lifetime. People would have died, people would have been born, a different generation. People didn't live, necessarily, for forty years in those days. And arriving in the Promised Land? We have no evidence of it whatsoever." Her bottom-line statement was, "I don't believe there was a single event that we can call the Exodus, archaeologically or historically."

As I interviewed expert after expert, time and again I heard there was either no physical evidence or any proof that was uncovered didn't match up with the Bible's apparent timeline. Feeling a deepening mix of shock and disappointment, I made a very real and deeply personal connection to the overall claims of Christianity from the Old Testament to the New Testament ...

If Moses didn't exist, then Jesus was a liar!

This means the Gospel itself was based on false claims, which would then mean there is no salvation, no real promise of Heaven. The ripple effects of this conclusion would create a tsunami of doubt and questions.

Now, just in case you are saying, "But wait, Tim, what's the big deal if there's no proof about Moses, the Exodus, and the Israelites in the Promised Land? What does that Old Testament history really have to do with Jesus anyway?" Well, with no proof of Moses, Joshua, Joseph, and the stories of the Israelites, what do we do with these New Testament verses quoting Christ or connecting His teachings and activities directly to Moses and the Prophets?

"Do not think that I have come to abolish the Law or the Prophets; I have not come to abolish them but to fulfill them." (Jesus in Matthew 5:17)

And Jesus said to him, "See that you say nothing to anyone, but go, show yourself to the priest and offer the gift that Moses commanded, for a proof to them." (Matthew 8:4)

And Pharisees came up and in order to test him asked, "Is it lawful for a man to divorce his wife?" He answered them, "What did Moses command you?" They said, "Moses allowed a man to write a certificate of divorce and to send her away." And Jesus said to them, "Because of your hardness of heart he wrote you this commandment." (Jesus in Mark 10:2–5)

"And as for the dead being raised, have you not read in the book of Moses, in the passage about the bush, how God spoke to him, saying, 'I am the God of Abraham, and the God of Isaac, and the God of Jacob'?" (Jesus in Mark 12:26)

And he was transfigured before them, and his face shone like the sun, and his clothes became white as light. And behold, there appeared to them Moses and Elijah, talking with him. (About Jesus in Matthew 17:2–3)

"He said to him, 'If they do not hear Moses and the Prophets, neither will they be convinced if someone should rise from the dead.'" (Jesus in Luke 16:31)

And beginning with Moses and all the Prophets, he interpreted to them in all the Scriptures the things concerning himself. (About Jesus in Luke 24:27)

Then he said to them, "These are my words that I spoke to you while I was still with you, that everything written about me in the Law of Moses and the Prophets and the Psalms must be fulfilled." (Jesus in Luke 24:44)

Have you ever seen the incredible amount of connection recorded in Scripture that Jesus made to Moses? I certainly hadn't. (Remember, I am not a Bible scholar, theologian, or pastor, but a filmmaker.) But I quickly realized that because of Jesus constantly connecting Himself to the Jewish forefathers of faith, His role in following after them, and His fulfilling God's plan, the connection of Moses and the Exodus of the Israelites being a historical reality is critical to whether our salvation is authentic or just a cruel fantasy!

If there was no Red Sea, then how was there a Resurrection? If there was no parting of the waters, then how could the stone be rolled away? If Christ said He came to fulfill what Moses started and there was no Moses, then was Christ who He claimed to be?

For me, standing in front of those quite confident nay-saying archaeologists, and now for us today, the question of "How important is it that these events were a historical reality?" becomes deeply personal. History meets biography! This connection is a linchpin that must be found. I now had a major motivation to connect evidence to faith.

What I believed about my future was dependent on what happened in the past.

Nothing But the Truth, So Help Me, God

For over 1,500 years, Western civilization accepted the Bible as being true, with the assumption being made that, once discovered, scientific evidence would back up the words of Scripture. But then a corner was turned and the paradigm shifted. After the 1950s, skepticism grew when archaeologists found mounting evidence contradicting the early history of the Bible.

Today, with real-time news feeds and social media platforms flowing moment by moment from all over the world, we continually take in information at light speed. Fifteen minutes is no longer a window for fame but simply old news. Due to this massive consumption that is akin to drinking from a fire hose, we hear a "fact" and take a complete stranger's word that it is true. We even take others' word for the truth in our own lives.

Today, truth is no longer a constant but a moving target; it is no longer a foundational element but an optional decoration. This was made quite real to me early on in one of the interviews I had arranged to film between radio talk show host Michael Medved and Rabbi David Wolpe, once named by Newsweek magazine as the most influential rabbi in America.

Medved began, "Rabbi Wolpe, one of the things that fascinated me is, about a decade ago, you gave a sermon in your synagogue, one of the largest conservative synagogues in the country; and that sermon became hugely controversial."

Wolpe nodded. "Yes."

Medved asked, "What did you say?"

Wolpe answered, "I said that the Exodus certainly didn't happen the way the Bible depicts it, assuming that it was a historical event in any description. But you also have to understand that your faith isn't based on splitting seas or archaeological digs. It's based on something much deeper."

Medved spurred on the dialogue, "Why did you say that?"

Wolpe replied, "I said it for two reasons. One was because I knew that these students and others would go off to college and hear people talk about biblical archaeology and comparative religion, and I wanted them to know that that was not a frightening topic. That belief was apart from what you uncover with a spade. The second part of it was, if you make a historical claim, then you have to be willing to let history look at it. What I meant to do was to try to tell people that no single fact or event was the pivot of faith. It was faith that was the pivot of faith."

Medved leaned forward and asserted, "I'm sure you heard from people who said, 'Wait a minute. You haven't considered this evidence or that evidence about the historicity of the Exodus.'"

Wolpe agreed.

Medved then asked, "Did any of those contacts lead you to reconsider your assumptions?"

"Well, they led me not so much to reconsider my assumptions that it didn't happen the way the Bible said. If you look at it scientifically, it's virtually indefensible to make the Bible's case. But I am persuaded that the Jewish people have some origin in the land of Egypt, although I also think that it is possible that the fleeing Jews from Egypt, when they came to Canaan, met up with people from the same background who were also an indigenous people in the land of Canaan from long before that. That is a possibility, but were you to ask me, 'Were Jews ever in Egypt?' I think I would put a lot of money on it that the Jews were in Egypt."

Medved countered, "But if these are not facts, if this is a fairy story, if this is somehow fabricated, doesn't that undermine its religious meaning? In other words, doesn't that change things?"

Wolpe answered, "The extent to which the Exodus story has a historical core is very hard to say, but my deeper conviction about it is that it's a story that whether it was true, it is true. And those are two different things."

Medved seemed unconvinced. "That seems to be evading."

Wolpe responded, "Well, there are things that aren't facts that can be truths."

Now, let's think about Wolpe's statements for a moment:

- "Whether [the Exodus] was true, it is true, and those are two different things."
- "There are things that aren't facts that can be truths."

Let's invert these sentences to dissect what the rabbi is communicating.

- Something doesn't have to be true to be truth.
- Truths do not have to be comprised of facts.

Might there be a connection between the scientific world, the religious paradigm, and the current culture joining forces to distance themselves from the truth of Scripture? We must ask, "What's the end game here?"

The Jesus & Jewish Juncture

As a Jewish leader, Rabbi Wolpe, as many of the archaeologists I inter-viewed, would be focused on the Torah—the first five books of the Bible.

In the days when the Bible was written, young Jewish boys were required to memorize the Torah—verbatim. (Yes, every verse of every chapter of all

five books!) When the appointed time came for a young man to be tested, a rabbi would ask him to quote random passages of text. He would also ask for the context in and around certain passages, so this requirement wasn't simply about memorization but knowing the Scripture by heart, having understanding of the meaning, not just storing facts in the mind and regurgitating them from the mouth.

After the test was completed, if the young man did not show both skill and passion for the Torah, he was encouraged to find a common trade to make a living. If he was deemed to be adept and agile with the Scripture, the rabbi would invite him to "Come and follow me," meaning the opportunity was given to live with him and become like him. This was the protocol and procedure for inaugurating a new generation of rabbis.

This Jewish concept shines new light on the day Jesus came upon some fishermen, young Jewish men who had obviously "flunked" the rabbi exam. But the Rabbi didn't test them; He called them. What these men did not yet know was that, down the road, a test greater than most men would ever endure was coming for each one of them, straight from the hand and heart of God Himself.

While walking by the Sea of Galilee, he saw two brothers, Simon (who is called Peter) and Andrew his brother, casting a net into the sea, for they were fishermen. And he said to them, "Follow me, and I will make you fishers of men." Immediately they left their nets and followed him. (Matthew 4:18–20)

Have you ever wondered, as I had, why these men would respond so quickly and appear to react impulsively to Jesus' invitation? A Rabbi of great reputation had called them. No one in that day would have seen that coming!

Jesus was the Connector of the Torah (God's history with man) to the New Testament (God's redemption of man). The threads of validity of the Scripture run deep from the time of Moses to the days of Jesus right up to today. This is why the very concept of salvation through the cross is threatened if the Torah is a collection of fables and legends.

When scientists and archaeologists began releasing information that what was being uncovered and discovered in the ground wasn't matching up to the pages of biblical history, right up to the events of today when God is being systematically removed and legislated from our culture, a very real crisis of faith develops for those who want to believe in the God of the Bible.

This dilemma drove me to spend twelve years researching, interviewing, and filming, doing investigative journalism to find real answers. No, I never picked up a shovel to dig in the dirt of the Middle East or the Holy Land, but I certainly excavated truckloads of information from some of today's most renowned experts. I dug deep for over a decade to find the truth.

In order for you to understand this journey you are now taking with me, it is crucial you fully understand what was—and is—at stake. Take a look at this passage from Hebrews that quotes Jeremiah 31:31–34, yet another merger between the days of the early Church and the forerunners of the faith.

"Behold, the days are coming, declares the Lord, when I will establish a new covenant with the house of Israel and with the house of Judah, not like the covenant that I made with their fathers on the day when I took them by the hand to bring them out of the land of Egypt. For they did not continue in my covenant, and so I showed no concern for them, declares the Lord. For this is the covenant that I will make with the house of Israel after those days, declares the Lord: I will put my laws into their minds, and write them on their hearts, and I will be their God, and they shall be my people. And they shall not teach, each one his neighbor and each one his brother, saying, 'Know the Lord,' for they shall all know me, from the least of them to the greatest. For I will be merciful toward their iniquities, and I will remember their sins no more." (Hebrews 8:8–12)

God took Israel by the hand to bring them out of Egypt but now enters our hearts to lead us out of sin. God wrote His Law on tablets, but now He writes it on our hearts. God placed the Law in Moses' hands, but He now transforms our minds with His precepts. God, through Christ, took the Law out of the hands of a select few and offered His love to all. No more animals must die on the altar, for His Son, the Lamb, died so God could "establish a new covenant" and "remember their sins no more."

So is God's Word a wondrous fantasy or His personal letter? Are we reading far-fetched fiction or faithful facts? My own crisis of belief drove me to find the answers for myself, but, over time, I was also on this journey so I could share my story with you.

 Now if Christ is proclaimed as raised from the dead, how can some of you say that there is no resurrection of the dead? But if there is no resurrection of the dead, then not even Christ has been raised. And if Christ has not been raised, then our preaching is in vain and your faith is in vain.

(1 Corinthians 15:12–14)

Chapter 1 Discussion Questions

1. Why do you suppose growing into adulthood often seems to invite increasing doubt and questions regarding faith and spiritual matters?

2. Discuss the Moses-to-Jesus connection, particularly in light of the Scriptures listed on pages 25-26.

3. What do you suppose drove Tim, a filmmaker and not a theologian or an archaeologist, to launch out on such a difficult journey, seeking answers to these questions?

4. Discuss this statement: "What I believed about my future was dependent on what happened in the past." How does the past continually impact our future?

5. Discuss this statement: "Today, truth is no longer a constant but a moving target; it is no longer a foundational element but an optional decoration." Agree or disagree? Why?

6. Discuss Rabbi Wolpe's statements: "Whether [the Exodus] was true, it is true, and those are two different things," and "There are things that aren't facts that can be truths." How do teachings from religious leaders such as this affect our world?

7. Regarding Jesus' calling of His disciples as a Rabbi, how do you think this concept affected the common people's perceptions of Him? What about the religious leaders' perceptions?

8. Does it surprise you that for the past sixty plus years, science and the early history in the Bible have not lined up? Why or why not? How does this impact your personal faith?

9. We each have a different perspective of the Bible, depending on our past and current paradigm. How can this diversity inspire and grow us rather than divide and separate us?

10. Regarding the closing passage (1 Corinthians 15:12–14), why do you think so much of our faith is dependent on the validity of the Resurrection of Christ?

Notes:

....

....

....

....

....

....

....

 **CHAPTER 2**

Secrets in the Sand

You must stick to your conviction, but be ready to abandon your assumptions.
— Denis Waitley [4]

Throughout the ages, all great stories have had a plot with a seemingly in-surmountable conflict. My own journey came to center around one such dilemma with a singular character. Not God or Moses or the Israelites, but a king—the king of Egypt, Ramesses II.

Ramesses II (conventionally dated to the 13th century BC) was a pha-raoh of the New Kingdom who ruled a grand empire including a city that bore his name. In modern culture, we are most familiar with this famous pharaoh from the classic Cecil B. DeMille film The Ten Commandments (1956) where Charlton Heston, portraying Moses, takes on Yul Brynner, evoking Ramesses. Disney's animated film The Prince of Egypt (1998) con-tinued the same trend, and Sir Ridley Scott, the director of the 2014 film Exodus: Gods and Kings, also carried on this concept.

With each re-telling and repetition, connecting this particular pharaoh to the Exodus was further ingrained into modern history as an apparent in-disputable fact. But was it? Just because influential people keep repeating the same information doesn't necessarily make it true. And why was this concept being repeated by so many? This is one of the central points of the issue. The Bible states that Joseph the great-grandson of Abraham was sold as a slave to Egypt, where he rose to become second-in-command and invited his father Jacob and his entire family to live in that land. So, in order for the Exodus to be true, there needs to be Israelites in Egypt, as well as big troubles brought on by the Ten Plagues. If experts claim there is no evidence for these things during Ramesses' reign, then why is seemingly everyone so persistent that he was that particular pharaoh?

There is one passage in the Bible that leads scientists, historians, and theologians alike to make the link between Ramesses and the time of the Exodus:

> *Now there arose a new king over Egypt, who did not know Joseph. And he said to his people, "Behold, the people of Israel are too many and too mighty for us. Come, let us deal shrewdly with them, lest they multiply, and, if war breaks out, they join our enemies and fight against us and escape from the land." Therefore they set taskmasters over them to afflict them with heavy burdens.* **They built for Pharaoh store cities, Pithom and Raamses.** *But the more they were oppressed, the more they multiplied and the more they spread abroad. And the Egyptians were in dread of the people of Israel. So they ruthlessly made the people of Israel work as slaves and made their lives bitter with hard service, in mortar and brick, and in all kinds of work in the field. In all their work they ruthlessly made them work as slaves. (Exodus 1:8–14)*

Most scholars date the Exodus to the time of Pharaoh Ramesses II because of the mention of the city of Raamses in this passage. Raamses is one of the alternate spellings for Ramesses. They choose this pharaoh because his grandfather, Ramesses I, was a very minor pharaoh who only reigned around two years and is not known for any significant construction. In contrast, Ramesses II was considered to be the greatest builder of all the kings of Egypt, even erecting a huge city named after him.

Wouldn't it be a reasonable and logical assumption that an entire nation of slaves could be responsible for the free and forced construction of all these grand sites?

Always Have Been, Always Will Be

In continuing my quest to link Egyptian history to the Bible's timeline, I decided to travel to Chicago to interview Professor James Hoffmeier, one of the few Egyptologists who has written extensively on the biblical Exodus. I asked him, "Why is it that so many people hold to the Ramesses Exodus Theory?"

Hoffmeier shared, "Key to that theory is the building of the city of Ramesses mentioned in Exodus 1:11. The Hebrews are making bricks to build this city of Ramesses or to construct the storage facilities of Ramesses. This important city, which we know Ramesses II built, is being excavated even as we speak and continues to be studied. It has a very brief history. It was expanded into the world's largest city back in the 13th century BC. By around 1100 BC the city is gone. It has a very narrow history of no more than two hundred years. If this building project that the Israelites are involved in is Ramesses II's Delta residence, then we have no escape but to say that this is an important chronological marker and that the Exodus can only be somewhere in the 13th century BC."

I then asked Hoffmeier, "Lately the Bible has been greatly challenged by people like Israel Finkelstein. He claims that the 'Exodus did not happen in the way that it is described in the text.' Tell me what's going on here?"

Hoffmeier explained, "Well, there will always be those who challenge the Bible. There always have been; there always will be. And archaeologists have come to play an important role in challenging the Bible and in confirming the Bible at the same time. So we have these two competing views. The Bible, or any text or narrative we read, requires a certain amount of interpretation or sophistication in reading. Similarly, archaeological data is not neutral. It has to be read, it has to be interpreted, and on any kind of scientific data, there are going to be differences of perspective, differences of viewpoint of how one looks at things. I can look at the same thing and see something in a positive way, and somebody else can come at it from a different perspective and see it in a negative way. So one's assumptions influence greatly how one views archaeological data."

There's that word again … assumptions. Have you noticed how many times this keeps appearing?

In the Ground, No Evidence

On one of my trips to Egypt, I visited Mansour Boraik, Director General of Antiquities at the Karnak Temple Complex in Luxor, whom I asked, "The events of the Exodus—would they have been recorded in Egypt?"

"Never," Boraik replied emphatically. "The Egyptians never mentioned bad things in the reliefs of the temples."

I continued, "Can we find any evidence for the Exodus in Egypt?"

He cautiously yet firmly proceeded, "Nobody knows what the sands of Egypt can tell of secrets. Maybe in the excavations we will find some evidence, but so far there's not any documented evidence about the Exodus. We know the story from the holy books only. It's mentioned in the Holy Koran more than seven times. It's in the Holy Bible. But in the ground, we have no evidence. We think that it was during the Ramesside time. But nobody can tell exactly which pharaoh was the hero of the Exodus."

I smiled to myself at Boraik's comment that Pharaoh, not Moses, was "the hero of the Exodus." I wanted an Egyptian perspective and I certainly got one.

A Weak Affair

Early on, I heard about the thirty-year archaeological work of Austrian Manfred Bietak from the University of Vienna, one of the world's most respected Egyptologists. He was on-site at the location of the ancient city of Ramesses, specifically at the site of Avaris. In the ground, this city of

Avaris lies directly below the southern sector of Ramesses. Commonly, cities were built on top of past cities, explaining why this layered phenomenon of discovery occurs. A city and a people that appeared to match the biblical story had been uncovered underneath. The film team and I traveled to this location on the eastern Nile Delta.

Bietak was limited on time but graciously gave me a brief explanation of what his team had found: "We uncovered the remains of a huge town of two hundred and fifty hectares with a population of approximately twenty-five thousand to thirty thousand individuals. These were people who have originated from Canaan, Syria-Palestine. Originally they may have come here as subjects of the Egyptian crown or with the blessing of the Egyptian crown. Obviously, this town enjoyed something like a special status, like a free zone, something like that."

This sounded exactly like the Bible! Pharaoh had given his blessing by allowing the early Israelites to settle freely in the best part of Egypt. There, they and their flocks prospered and multiplied greatly. In my own research, I had learned this city of foreigners had a long history in the midst of Egyptian territory with no walls or defenses, being allowed to develop by the government. So I then asked him the burning question, "Could these foreigners be the early Israelites?"

He cautiously replied, "We have some evidence of shepherds. We find again and again in this area, pits with goats and sheep. So we know shepherds, probably Bedouins, with huge herds roamed around this. But to connect this with the proto-Israelites is a very weak affair. According to my opinion, the settlement of the proto-Israelites in Canaan only happened from the 12th century BC onwards."

A "weak affair"? I was stunned! This was not at all what I had expected to hear him say. I thought this was a new discovery, a new connection to the story in the Bible. My mind desperately tried to comprehend what I had just heard. So I continued, "Why couldn't these be the Israelites when they match the Bible's story so well?"

Bietak repeated, "According to my opinion, the settlement of the proto-Israelites in Canaan only happened from the 12th century BC onwards."

What the archaeologist was saying was that the physical evidence of these people at Avaris was centuries too early to be connected to the Exodus. He believes the earliest settlement of the Israelites in the land of Canaan didn't happen until after the time of Ramesses II. So, I had gone to the very location where the events of the Exodus were said to have happened and stood before one of a handful of men in the world who could tell me if there was any evidence for the Israelites in Egypt. He told me in an expert's opinion that there was none. The implications were profound, because no Israelites in Egypt means no Exodus. And no Exodus means that the foundational story of Judaism is based on a myth.

For Christians then, if these events never took place, it means that Jesus Christ and the writers of the New Testament were also wrong, since they all accepted the historical reality of Moses and the Exodus, building their teachings on them.

For months after I returned home from Egypt, I replayed my interview with Bietak over and over in my head. I wanted to be open-minded, but as the reality of what he said set in, a cold chill came over me. All my life I had believed the Bible's stories to be true. I know that some people say you don't need any evidence, just faith. But if there's no hard evidence for any of it, had I believed in a lie all this time? What about my kids and grandkids? What should they put their faith in?

Definite physical evidence found that is deemed to be centuries too early for the Exodus, yet here was another expert refuting the connection to the scriptural timeline.

So, let's recap:

- Scientists, scholars, and movie moguls have carried on the idea that Ramesses II was the Pharaoh of the Exodus with little challenge.
- The interpretation of one Bible verse (Exodus 1:11) is used to date the Exodus in the view of most scholars.
- No one seems to be able to match up "evidence in the ground" with the timeline of the Bible. And, increasingly, they are no longer even caring to make the connection.

After traveling halfway around the world, I was now fighting an internal battle inside a crisis of faith.

Wall of Time

As I gathered more and more data in my research, I knew I needed some sort of physical timeline to visibly display and comprehensibly understand the combined factors of:

- What was popularly accepted by the experts
- What the Bible said
- My own findings

In short, I needed to marry up Scripture to history in a visual manner. After various failed attempts to create a model, with the help of my staff I finally arrived at what I logically named the "Wall of Time." Once the graphic image was "built," this wall stretched back to the earliest point of civilization.

On the first level, I placed Egyptian history, and on the second level, the events recorded in the Bible. At the base was a timeline of actual or BC dates, an immovable foundation to gauge the markers of history with great pylons marking every one thousand years.

Scholars who study this area of the world have created varied approaches for dividing its history. Their first approach identifies the great kingdoms of ancient Egypt. Over the course of two thousand years, Egypt experienced three of these periods, each lasting for hundreds of years. The first period was the Old Kingdom with its great pyramids of stone. Next was the Middle Kingdom, the high point of art and literature. Finally, the New Kingdom emerged with its vast empires that dominated foreign lands.

Each of these three great periods of power was followed by a dark age, a stretch of time in which scholars have found less clearly defined activity in the archaeology. These dark ages are known as the First, Second, and Third Intermediate Periods, when the power of Egypt collapsed and the nation experienced many troubles. During these times, the pharaohs usually lacked the wealth and stability to build great tombs, monuments, or temples.

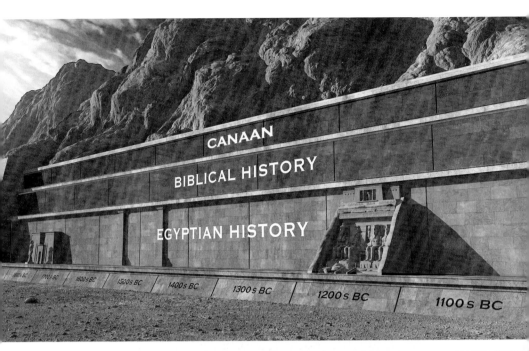

Scholars break down time into smaller units by identifying the different dynasties that reigned over Egypt. A dynasty generally consisted of generations of pharaohs from the same family. For example, Ramesses I initiated the Nineteenth Dynasty. Next to reign was his son Seti I, who was followed by Ramesses I's grandson, Ramesses II. A total of thirty dynasties have been recognized, and each one of the three great kingdom periods included several of these powers that ruled a unified Egypt in succession. However, in the more chaotic Intermediate Periods, there could be multiple dynasties ruling at the same time in different regions of Egypt.

Working with BC dates was often confusing because they move in the opposite direction of AD dates. The farther back in time you go, the bigger the BC number. With AD dates, as you go farther back in time, the numbers get smaller. There is no year 0; 1 BC is followed by 1 AD.

The centerpiece of my investigation was that the Ramesses Exodus Theory placed the date for the Exodus at around 1250 BC. On the Wall of Time, I also placed the six steps of the biblical sequence running parallel to Egyptian history:

- Arrival (Abraham's descendants come to Egypt)
- Multiplication (Israel's rapid population growth)
- Slavery (Israel's forced bondage by Pharaoh)
- Judgment (God's judgment upon Egypt by the plagues)
- Exodus (God's deliverance of Israel out of Egypt)
- Conquest (Israel's return to God's Promised Land in Canaan)

If the Exodus really happened, then you would naturally and logically expect some evidence would have been left behind in Egypt and could therefore be found. After all, a massive people group quickly left a nation en masse, much like a neighborhood of people evacuating their homes in the middle of the night. Due to the suddenness of the exit, plenty of evidence that they existed there would be left behind. This phenomenon would certainly be true for an entire nation of people.

My team agreed that by breaking down the big questions into these six primary steps, we would have a much more precise tool to test any evidence found. For an Exodus theory to match the Bible, all the criteria would need to be fulfilled.

Science solves problems by looking for patterns of evidence—hence the film title—and a truly objective approach will look for those no matter where they exist. I set out to see whether we could match these steps and attempt to find exactly where they were in ancient history.

Know What You Know

What about you? Where are you on the Wall of Time? Where do you come in? From your birth to today:

- Where is your arrival into a spiritual journey?
- What events and people helped you to expand in your understanding of the Gospel and draw closer in your walk with God?
- When did you first realize you were in bondage to the slavery of sin?
- When did you learn you could escape the judgment of sin by accepting Christ's substitution for your own death?
- When was your exodus from the imprisonment of the flesh to freedom in Christ?
- When did you first arrive in the Promised Land—the Kingdom of God on Earth—the precursor to Heaven?

Let me ask a sobering question. Is it a futile exercise to read a book on the search for the evidence of the Exodus and miss the God of the Promised Land? The film *Patterns of Evidence* tells the story of my twelve-year journey. The goal of this book is to turn the experience over to you. What does this grand historical account in Scripture mean in your life? If the God of the Bible is real and this is true, then you are indeed very much in this story, as am I.

Ironically, since the 1950s when archaeological data (or lack of it) began to sway people away from the biblical account, our mechanized and fast-paced culture has increasingly drawn a massive amount of truth from its own collaborated assumptions in most areas of the culture. This has certainly accelerated with the Internet age where Wi-Fi exists even where food does not.

In science, the goal is to find truths by following the patterns of evidence. If the evidence is strong enough, this will lead to a proper conclusion. Throughout such a process, one should not rely on presuppositions—ideas the researcher has made up his or her mind about before any evidence is considered.

Here are the critical questions I had to face—queries all Christians, along with those who are spiritually searching, must answer:

- What do I believe about the God of the Bible?
- Do I believe the Bible is the Word of God?
- Do I rely on anyone else's information to form my personal beliefs? If so, who? If so, why?
- What assumptions am I making regarding my faith using someone else's truth?

In my journey to find biblical evidence in the physical world, I had to face my own faith inside my spiritual world.

The Apostle Paul in his New Testament letters constantly challenged and tested those followers in the brand-new churches to know what they believed about the Triune God—Father, Son, and Holy Spirit. He knew these new "Bodies of Christ" were only as strong as the individual members. Paul was motivated and driven by his own indisputable evidence after Jesus appeared post-Resurrection to him on the road to Damascus. Regardless of who might disbelieve or discount his experience, the rest of his life was based on that event with Christ. Like Paul, there is a point in each of our lives where we must capture our own moment to know what we know about Christ. Or we simply dismiss it and walk away.

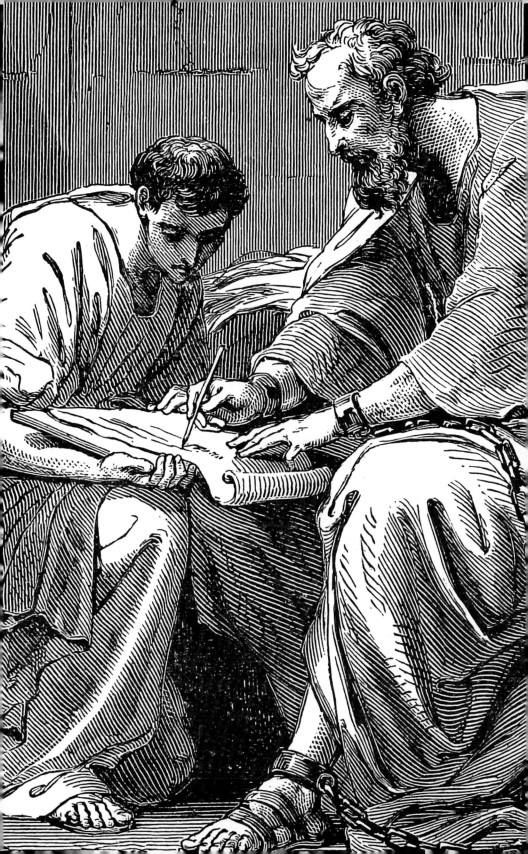

And I was with you in weakness and in fear and much trembling, and my speech and my message were not in plausible words of wisdom, but in demonstration of the Spirit and of power, so that your faith might not rest in the wisdom of men but in the power of God. Yet among the mature we do impart wisdom, although it is not a wisdom of this age or of the rulers of this age, who are doomed to pass away. But we impart a secret and hidden wisdom of God, which God decreed before the ages for our glory. (1 Corinthians 2:3–7)

God's wisdom is "secret and hidden" much like my uphill battle to find His patterns of evidence in the sands of time. Our faith cannot be in the knowledge of men but in the power of God. Such is not wisdom of the ages, but wisdom from the deep places of the Father Himself.

I had to fully rely upon God's power to sift through the vast knowledge of brilliant men and women who claimed to know the truth about the history of the Israelites. I came to see that my own spiritual growth comes not from following popular ideas or traditions, not by making assumptions, but by exploring and examining for myself what is true.

He who descended is the one who also ascended far above all the heavens, that he might fill all things.) And he gave the apostles, the prophets, the evangelists, the shepherds and teachers, to equip the saints for the work of ministry, for building up the body of Christ, until we all attain to the unity of the faith and of the knowledge of the Son of God, to mature manhood, to the measure of the stature of the fullness of Christ, so that we may no longer be children, tossed to and fro by the waves and carried about by every wind of doctrine, by human cunning, by craftiness in deceitful schemes. Rather, speaking the truth in love, we are to grow up in every way into him who is the head, into Christ. (Ephesians 4:10–15)

Paul encouraged the believers in Ephesus to actually experience unity, knowledge, maturity, stability, truth, and love that only Christ can give. Not simply believe in the concepts, but practice them firsthand!

I faced this same difficult choice of accepting others' truth or investigating for myself. As my faith was challenged and stretched, this demanded I constantly seek out my own experiences—as in my many trips and interviews, filming, and countless hours of research to bring "unity," "knowledge," and the "truth" to this volatile and divisive subject of the Exodus.

Now I rejoice in my sufferings for your sake, and in my flesh I am filling up what is lacking in Christ's afflictions for the sake of his body, that is, the church, of which I became a minister according to the stewardship from God that was given to me for you, to make the word of God fully known, the mystery hidden for ages and generations but now revealed to his saints. To them God chose to make known how great among the Gentiles are the riches of the glory of this mystery, which is Christ in you, the hope of glory. Him we proclaim, warning everyone and teaching everyone with all wisdom, that we may present everyone mature in Christ. For this I toil, struggling with all his energy that he powerfully works within me. (Colossians 1:24–29)

Paul sacrificed his very body so that each believer might be presented "mature in Christ."

My calling spanned years of research, travel into difficult locations, and many types of risks. The goal of unraveling the truth about the Exodus seemed impossible at times. The key for me was being freed from previous assumptions to explore new proof and its possible connection to biblical events. As these associations were made, I could see how this pattern of evidence could "make the word of God fully known."

A Hill to Die On

You may ask why I have now taken you from Moses to Christ to Paul? The succession of lead characters from the Old to the New Testament has a lineage we must connect, for they each built upon the past to bring about the future of the faith!

The early Church was fully aware they had come from the legacy of Abraham, Isaac, and Jacob. The Law of Moses was ingrained in their faith paradigm. All this connected to Jesus, in whose hands the early disciples placed their very lives. Then came Paul, theological assassin turned church planter, to spread the Gospel and build up the Body of Christ.

As Christians, we come from a long history of followers who had to know exactly what they believed because their faith was forged in the fires of persecution and hardship, lest they fall away and the Church die before it even had time to be embedded into history. No one would walk through the storms that the early disciples of Jesus did after His Ascension for mere assumptions and taken-for-granted traditions.

As I was challenged to invest years of time, energy, and money into my own journey following God's patterns of evidence, so I want to inspire you in these pages to follow Christ and Paul's challenge to know what you believe, live deeply in those truths, and walk in maturity inside your own journey with Jesus. Know what you know, as I was challenged to do and still am each day.

We must not simply strive to be like everyone else, but to be like Christ. God meets each of us in our own crisis of faith where He not only works on us but in us and then through us! We must make no assumptions. Even when the facts are hidden in the sands of time, we must discover them for ourselves. We will only die on the hills where we actually own truth.

 So Jesus said to the Jews who had believed him, "If you abide in my word, you are truly my disciples, and you will know the truth, and the truth will set you free." (John 8:31–32)

Chapter 2 Discussion Questions

1.   Why do you think so many unchallenged opinions and convenient assumptions are passed through our culture as "truths"?

2.   How do you think any lack of personal investigation on our part impacts our view of the Bible and its truths?

3.   Discuss Professor Hoffmeier's statement: "Well, there will always be those who challenge the Bible. There always have been; there always will be." Why is Scripture so controversial?

4.   Tim faced so many different opinions in his research. How do we allow others' opinions to factor into our own approach to the Word of God?

5.   Tim's "Wall of Time" method actually mirrors any Bible study method—existing expert (theological) information, the Bible's actual words, and our own findings. Discuss these factors. How can we use these to grow in maturity? How can these become imbalanced? How do we find what works for us to truly grow spiritually?

6.   Discuss the four critical questions on page 48. Share only what you are comfortable disclosing, while being as transparent as possible.

7.   Consider this statement: "Like Paul, there is a point in each of our lives where we must capture our own moment to know what we know about Christ." Would anyone like to share that process in your own life?

8.   Regarding 1 Corinthians 2:3–7 and Ephesians 4:10–15, why do you think Paul continually encouraged actual experience in the work of Christ? What was his goal?

9. What can we glean from Colossians 1:24–29 to challenge and motivate us today?

10. What are some practical ways we can make less assumptions and more carefully examine our faith so we can "know the truth, and the truth will set [us] free?"

Notes:

....

....

....

....

....

....

....

....

....

....

CHAPTER 3

Valley Days & Victory Laps

The essential thing 'in heaven and earth' is that there should be a long obedience in the same direction; there thereby results, and has always resulted in the long run, something which has made life worth living.
— *Friedrich Nietzsche* [5]

As Christians we try to live out a calling from God on our lives in some form or another. We all find ourselves longing to know it, sometimes resting in it, sometimes failing, but always hopeful that we are truly on the path and in the plan. Along the way, we all have mountaintop moments and then "valley of the shadow of death" encounters as well. If we're all honest, the "valley days" seem to far outnumber the victory laps. But, unfortunately, we tend to grow far faster and most efficiently from enduring our burdens than from basking in blessings. And then when a breakthrough does come, it seems so much sweeter.

So many times on my own journey, whether sifting through footage in Minneapolis or sitting across from a scholar in Egypt, I had the constant temptation, or what some might call just good common sense, to stop and go back to my life as it was before this giant game of hide-and-seek ever began. But "something" just kept driving me on. I couldn't quit.

In those moments of weariness and wavering determination, we find ourselves in such great company. The "something" is exactly what drove Noah to finish the ark, Abraham to leave for the "land he knew not of," Moses to go up onto Mount Sinai, Joshua to cross the Jordan, and, eventually, Jesus to endure the agony of the cross. There is a grand thread of faith running through both history and hearts, tying us to God, knitting us into one another, and drawing us all to the big picture and the grand plan.

While we often shy away from counting ourselves among these heroes of the faith, God makes it abundantly clear that our lives and callings are just as crucial to our generation on His behalf. We come from a strong legacy of faith followers driven to carry on the same task God lays before us today. Because the "something" is Someone, and, regardless of popular opinion or scholarly counsel, we know this because we know Him. Mountain or valley, burden or blessing, big or small, majestic or mundane—if God is for us, who can be against us (Romans 8:31)?

> *Therefore, since we are surrounded by so great a cloud of witnesses, let us also lay aside every weight, and sin which clings so closely, and let us run with endurance the race that is set before us, looking to Jesus, the founder and perfecter of our faith, who for the joy that was set before him endured the cross, despising the shame, and is seated at the right hand of the throne of God. Consider him who endured from sinners such hostility against himself, so that you may not grow weary or fainthearted. (Hebrews 12:1–3)*

Jesus endured so that "you may not grow weary or fainthearted." The "you" is us! This inspiring passage has spurred on millions of believers over centuries to stick to Plan A and to not only not quit but to "run with endurance." Even when you're sitting in Egypt, wondering how you got there and what to do next.

On my Exodus quest, I found myself at a crossroads where I needed a turning point—or better yet, a tipping point. I was stuck inside the investigation of a story, which so far had no supporting evidence. I was at a place of desperately seeking a break to come my way. And, as God so often does, one finally ... slowly ... began to show itself.

Replacing Ramesses

On a trip to Egypt, I spoke on-site with one of America's leading Egyptologists, Professor Kent Weeks, who rediscovered what is known as KV5, the tomb of the sons of Ramesses II in the Valley of the Kings. Seated at the base of an ancient monument, I asked, "Can you tell me who Ramesses II was?"

He leaned back and said, "That's a question that has perplexed Egyptologists for a long time, and there are several reasons for this. Partly because Ramesses II lived into his eighties at a time when the average life expectancy of an Egyptian was in the mid-thirties. He ruled Egypt for sixty-seven years. That means probably two generations of Egyptians had never known another pharaoh. During his lifetime, he managed to do a lot of things that certainly justify his being called Ramesses the Great. He was a military leader, conducted numerous battles, extended and maintained the borders of Egypt well beyond the Nile Valley."

I prodded, "Ramesses had an empire. Is that what you are saying?"

Weeks agreed, "Indeed he did, and it was one of the economic mainstays of the country. During his lifetime Egypt was remarkably well off economically, and that meant, among other things, Ramesses could engage in elaborate building programs. I doubt there's a monument that was standing in his reign that he didn't add to or usurp. And there are certainly numerous other monuments that he built from scratch. We're sitting in one, the Ramesseum, his mortuary—a memorial temple."

I then asked, "Could Ramesses II potentially have been the pharaoh of the Exodus story?"

Once again, I saw the word *Exodus* raise a thoughtful brow and evoke a cautious tone, as Weeks explained, "This is a real can of worms, this question of who was the pharaoh of the Exodus, and there have probably been as many suggestions put forth as there are Egyptologists and ancient historians

to suggest them. And the reason for the confusion, or the lack of agreement I should say, is because there is simply so little evidence to go on. There's no mention of this in ancient Egyptian sources, and you might say, 'Well, why would there be?' Why would the Egyptians carve on their temple walls for all eternity a note saying, 'Yes, there were big problems in town. We suffered a great loss, or we lost a battle.' These are not the things you want to inscribe in perpetuity."

As Weeks went on, he said what was to become a game-changer moment for me, "But Ramesses II is the pharaoh of the Exodus? How can we prove that? Chronology doesn't really help. The chronology of Egypt is still a bit ambiguous. Correlations between Egyptian chronology and that of other cultures in the ancient Near East is even more confusing. We don't know precisely when the Exodus happened. Some people say it was Ramesses II. It makes nice theater because he was a great, powerful ruler. Everybody knows his name. He built fantastic monuments. Everything really is appealing to have him be the one to choose."

I pressed further, "Because he'd be a very large opponent, wouldn't he?"

"He would be indeed," Weeks agreed.

"And he had declared himself a god," I added.

"Exactly right again," he answered. "So, yeah, pick Ramesses II as the pharaoh of the Exodus, but other Egyptologists, other ancient historians disagree. Any pharaoh reigning during that time could be the pharaoh of the Exodus … if we can prove there even was an Exodus."

Even though Professor Weeks ended exactly with the same tone as so many of my interviews had, there was a new thought introduced here: If Ramesses wasn't the Pharaoh of the Exodus, then who was?

Looking for the Exodus in a different time or reign could be the solution. Maybe Ramesses—not the Exodus—is actually the real problem here? I felt a moment of "what if?" that I was certainly very grateful to entertain.

This connected to something Mansour Boraik had spoken to me. In his strong, distinct style, he made this statement regarding the work of historical investigation: "Scientifically you have to open your mind to all the opinions. Read it by yourself. Don't let anybody affect what you believe. But also on the other hand, you have to accept the other opinions. Your opinions are not always the right opinions. You have to accept other opinions and debate with me. Discuss. You can convince me, or shall I convince you? Leave it to the public to judge. We have a myth. We have a story. It's in the holy books. Who knows? And then you will come with a conclusion, and this conclusion will be in front of the public. The public can judge."

In essence, he was encouraging me to consider everyone's opinions, but to *follow* my conviction and *arrive* at my own conclusion. And maybe, in the end, my research regarding the Bible would be found *authentic*.

And He Believed

But I must constantly return to my roots that, while I am looking for evidence, this is not simply about personal opinions or the words of men. Let's go back to where this all began, in Genesis 15.

> *After these things the word of the Lord came to Abram in a vision: "Fear not, Abram, I am your shield; your reward shall be very great." But Abram said, "O Lord God, what will you give me, for I continue childless, and the heir of my house is Eliezer of Damascus?" And Abram said, "Behold, you have given me no offspring, and a member of my household will be my heir." And behold, the word of the Lord came to him: "This man shall not be your heir; your very own son shall be your heir." And he brought him outside and said, "Look toward heaven, and number the stars, if you are able to number them." Then he said to him, "So shall your offspring be." And he believed the Lord, and he counted it to him as righteousness. And he said to him, "I am the Lord who brought you out from Ur of the Chaldeans to give you this land to possess." ... Then the Lord said to Abram, "Know for certain that your offspring will be sojourners in a land that is not theirs and will be servants there, and they will be afflicted for four hundred years. But I will bring judgment on the nation that they serve, and afterward they shall come out with great possessions. As for you, you shall go to your fathers in peace; you shall be buried in a good old age. And they shall come*

back here in the fourth generation, for the iniquity of the Amorites is not yet complete."… On that day the Lord made a covenant with Abram, saying, "To your offspring I give this land, from the river of Egypt to the great river, the river Euphrates, the land of the Kenites, the Kenizzites, the Kadmonites, the Hittites, the Perizzites, the Rephaim, the Amorites, the Canaanites, the Girgashites and the Jebusites." (Genesis 15:1–7, 13–16, 18–21)

This Bible passage is known as God's Covenant with Abraham. This account written in Scripture is not intended to be personal conjecture, not a whimsical tale of fantasy, but an actual conversation written down between God and man. The Great I Am was making big promises. He was telling Abraham not only *his* future, but the future of *his nation* as well.

In this passage lies one of the most amazing phrases in the Bible: "And he believed the Lord." Imagine this … God tells a man to look up into the clear night sky and that from him will come more children throughout the generations than the number of stars he can see. And Abraham's response to this unfathomable statement? He simply believed it *was* true and that it *would* be true.

My heart was leading me, confirming to me, to know this story has always been true, is true, and will continue to be true. Was my investigation beginning to open a window that science's assumptions, assignments, and placements over the past fifty plus years *might* be wrong? I too must listen to what God told Abraham and simply believe Him. Let it be said of me: And Tim believed the Lord.

Looking once again to the book of Hebrews for strength …

Remember your leaders, those who spoke to you the word of God. Consider the outcome of their way of life, and imitate their faith. Jesus Christ is the same yesterday and today and forever. Do not be led away by diverse and strange teachings, for it is good for the heart to be strengthened by grace. (Hebrews 13:7–9)

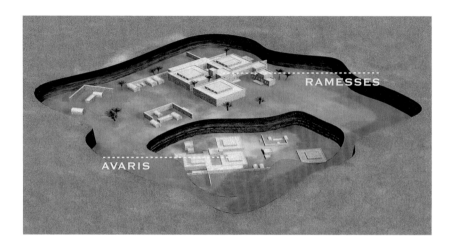

Living out your faith while being constantly hit in the face with a barrage of reality is one of the toughest aspects of life. But that is exactly why it is indeed "good for the heart to be strengthened by grace."

A Biblical Quest

While we often tend to feel that God works slowly, there are times when His help comes like a bolt out of the blue. This was one of those moments for me.

Back at the editing bay in my office, I was repeatedly listening to the scene where Manfred Bietak was saying there was no evidence for the Israelites in Egypt. I was gripped with his statement. Suddenly, I had the distinct sense that I was to stop and go to my office. Once there I "happened" to notice a book on my shelf that I had been given by a friend but had yet to read: *Pharaohs and Kings: A Biblical Quest* by David Rohl.

Rohl, whom I quoted in chapter 1, is an Egyptologist, author, and historian—and agnostic. He believes the Bible stories are authentic history but remains unconvinced that the God they are written about is real. Rohl asserts there is substantial archaeological evidence to support the existence of Joseph, Jacob, and the Hebrews. But he states, "As an agnostic, I don't *need* these stories to be true."

Rohl was coming from a completely different perspective in his motivation. I had been raised to believe these stories were real, had come to a place of question and doubt, and was looking, futilely up to this moment, for any proof. He, on the other hand, read the stories as solely history, and, over many years of on-site investigation and research, was convinced he had found evidence that these people not only existed but *when* they existed. Now there's a plot twist!

Rohl believes that many Egyptologists have missed evidence for the Exodus because they have been looking in the wrong time period. While most think the event happened in Egypt's New Kingdom, he asserts it happened earlier in the Middle Kingdom. I couldn't help but feel some hope that maybe speaking with Rohl would lead me to a new place in this search for answers.

In one early interview, I asked him about Bietak, knowing my encounter with the Austrian archaeologist at the dig had created my biggest roadblock. Rohl began, "Manfred Bietak is probably one of the greatest archaeologists alive today. And he's dug up one of the most important sites in the eastern Delta, a city called Avaris, which is in the land of Goshen, as the Bible calls it. And I believe this is the place where Joseph and his brethren lived."

I then told him, "I went to see Manfred Bietak, and that's not what he said. He's saying there's no evidence of this in the time of Ramesses."

Undaunted, Rohl continued, "Exactly right. Most scholars will say if you look at the city of Ramesses, there are no Semites. But dig down a little bit deeper and you do find a city full of Asiatics." (Semitic people, or Western Asiatics, were the cultural group to which the Israelites belonged.)

Now quite surprised, I asked him to clarify. "Yes, but it appears the Bible says in Exodus 1:11 that this happened at the time of Ramesses. What are *you* saying?"

"I'm saying that this particular mention of the city of Ramesses—the building of Ramesses—is what we call an anachronism. It's something that's been added into the text later by an editor. So what the editor is basically saying is, 'This is the *place* where the Israelites built the store city, and we know it today as Ramesses.'"

There are other examples of anachronisms found in the Bible. For example, the city of Dan mentioned in Genesis 14:14. The city was not actually called Dan at the time of Abraham. In Judges 18:29, we learn that the city was renamed at the time of Joshua—centuries after Abraham—and had formerly been called Laish. Yet there is no mention of Laish when the city is first mentioned in Genesis.

My understanding was that Rohl was saying the Bible's use of the word *Ramesses* might not be connected to a specific *date* but only to a *place*. I continued, "Okay, so the people would know the area, the region, and would have known what it was called in that day."

"The people of the Bible would've known where Ramesses was and where therefore their ancestors actually built the city. In the ancient times it was called Avaris," he stated.

An example in modern history books is the stating that Columbus discovered America, but it was not called by that name at the time he discovered it. The people in that day called this "the New World." The name "America" came about many years later. Yet we do not declare the modern textbooks wrong for calling it America, since we know it by the contemporary name.

Rohl continued his increasingly fascinating explanation, "Now, this Avaris is the city which lies under the biblical Ramesses of the New Kingdom—Avaris of the Middle Kingdom, the Thirteenth Dynasty. It lies underneath the city that's mentioned in the Bible. So when Bietak digs up a huge population of Semitic-speaking peoples with Semitic culture, living in this city of Avaris for several hundred years, and then at the end of the period these Semites all leave, depart with their belongings and abandon the city, whatever Manfred says, that to me sounds awfully like the Israelites."

After all the negative conclusions I'd gathered from other scholars, to finally hear of this potential connection between Joseph's family and the archaeological evidence was life-changing. Rohl was quite confident of his opinions, so could Avaris really be the place where the Israelites had lived? It seemed to be a possibility because it lies underneath the ruins of the city of Ramesses and would therefore be older.

But why was Bietak's interpretation so different? I challenged Rohl again,

"Well, what Bietak told me was that there was no connection."

Unmoved, he carried on, "Well, look at the evidence of what you've got here. Right at the beginning, in the heart of this tiny community of Avaris at the end of the Twelfth Dynasty, we see a Syrian house appear. The Austrians call them *Mittelsaal* houses. This type of house is found in north Syria, the area where Abraham came from. It's exactly the same style of house you'd expect Jacob to build for himself in Egypt. And we know that the Israelites sought their brides from Haran in that region. They all went back to get their brides from there. So, the culture that turns up in Egypt at the end of the Twelfth Dynasty seems to have come from north Syria originally."

This would mean that the culture seen at Avaris matches that of the early Israelites, so I asked, "Is there a connection with Joseph at Avaris?"

Rohl answered, "Well, after this house of Jacob—if we can call it that—is built, eventually it's flattened, and on top of it an Egyptian palace is constructed. The palace is classic Egyptian architecture this time, but the occupant was not Egyptian. The palace had courtyards, colonnades, and audience chambers. There was even a robing room. It obviously belonged to some high official of state who was very, very important to that state. Because when somebody gets a palace like this given to them, it means they've been honored for what they've done for the state. Now in the garden behind the palace, the archaeologists found twelve main graves with memorial chapels on top of them."

"Twelve graves?" I asked.

"Well, think about it. How many sons did Jacob have?" Rohl asked.

I answered, "He had twelve."

"How many tribes were there?"

Again, I answered, "Twelve tribes."

"Exactly. And what's also amazing is the palace had a façade, a portico with twelve pillars. So you've got twelve sons, twelve tribes, twelve pillars, and twelve tombs."

While Rohl certainly had my full attention, things were about to get even more interesting.

"Is that all a coincidence?" He paused and smiled. "Now, one of these twelve graves was very special because it was a pyramid tomb. This in itself is extraordinary because only pharaohs and queens had pyramid tombs at this time. Yet the person buried in this tomb was not a king. Even so, he was honored with a king's burial. And inside the chapel of the tomb was a statue. What we know from the statue is that this man had red hair, he had pale yellow skin, which is how Egyptians depicted northerners. He had a throw stick across his shoulder, a unique symbol of office made for this Asiatic official living in the land of Goshen. And on the back of his shoulder we see the faintest remains of paint, of colored stripes from a multicolored coat. And that matches exactly with the story of Joseph in the Bible. The multicolored coat is a gift, which shows that he was the favorite of the father. And it almost becomes his insignia, this coat. It's the thing we remember about him most of all."

So I asked, "Do you know of any other statues of a Semite of this kind in Egypt?"

Rohl, calm and confident, answered, "There is nothing else like this in the whole of Egyptian history … nothing at all."

Please allow me to sum up the fact that an agnostic Egyptologist is explaining to me that he believes wholeheartedly that what has been uncovered at Avaris—underneath Ramesses, the issue of Exodus 1:11—is the home of Jacob, the brothers, and the tomb of Joseph, right down to the detail of the multicolored coat.

With this single interview, I felt a change in the weather and my sails take on a fresh wind. What began with Professor Weeks raising question to popular belief on the pharaohs to Boraik's inspiration to keep pressing forward, and now to Rohl's interpretation of what Bietak had actually uncovered at Avaris, I could see a glimmer of light in the once pitch-dark tunnel.

Would more light come or would the darkness return? I had to find out, and I now had the fuel to keep going. Once again, I was drawn back to the writer to the Hebrews, the very descendants of these transplants in Avaris …

By faith we understand that the universe was created by the word of God, so that what is seen was not made out of things that are visible. (Hebrews 11:3)

The Bottom Line

I want to stop at this crossroads in my story for a moment. If you were with me on a scorching-hot day in Egypt, we'd sit down in the shade of a grand monument to visit a few minutes. The focus up to now has been on me in this journey. Now I want to turn it to you. Before we move on to see where Rohl's conclusions might take us, we must stop on the road to allow you to be certain of your own path.

Every time any of us hear the Gospel or the good news of Jesus, born out of the lineage of the many men and women of the Old Testament who trusted the Lord, we can learn something about what we believe and deepen in our own faith. But whether this is your first time or your ten-thousandth to read these words, there is a fresh start available every time, for that is the Father's heart for His children.

There is a God-shaped hole, or emptiness, inside each of us. We all try to fill this void in our own way. We try dysfunctional relationships, illicit sex, drugs, alcohol, money, materialism, and ten thousand other unhealthy habits. We can try to fill the chasm in our souls with a lot of things—even religion—but none of them give us real peace and contentment. We cannot see on our own that God Himself is the answer to our emptiness. His Spirit has to help us.

The Bible defines sin as attitudes, thoughts, and actions that displease God. Every person since Adam and Eve has had this problem. Even if we try really hard to be "good," we still make selfish decisions that are not pleasing to God.

In Paul's letter to the Roman church, he created a pattern of evidence laying out a path to salvation in Christ. For millions of people, these simple yet profound truths have led to new life.

For his invisible attributes, namely, his eternal power and divine nature, have been clearly perceived, ever since the creation of the world, in the things that have been made. So they are without excuse. For although they knew God, they did not honor him as God or give thanks to him, but they became futile in their thinking, and their foolish hearts were darkened. (Romans 1:20–21)

But now the righteousness of God has been manifested apart from the law, although the Law and the Prophets bear witness to it—the righteousness of God through faith in Jesus Christ for all who believe. For there is no distinction: for all have sinned and fall short of the glory of God, and are justified by his grace as a gift, through the redemption that is in Christ Jesus. (Romans 3:22–24)

But God shows his love for us in that while we were still sinners, Christ died for us. (Romans 5:8)

For the wages of sin is death, but the free gift of God is eternal life in Christ Jesus our Lord. (Romans 6:23)

Because, if you confess with your mouth that Jesus is Lord and believe in your heart that God raised him from the dead, you will be saved. For with the heart one believes and is justified, and with the mouth one confesses and is saved. (Romans 10:9–10)

For "everyone who calls on the name of the Lord will be saved." (Romans 10:13)

For from him and through him and to him are all things. To him be glory forever. Amen. (Romans 11:36)

I intentionally did not offer any explanation or thoughts in between these passages because they speak for themselves. The Holy Spirit can speak His truth to your spirit, as He once did mine. This is the truth of the Gospel. This is the pattern the Apostle Paul gave, but you, my friend, can be the evidence as am I. But God gives you the choice.

For I am not ashamed of the gospel, for it is the power of God for salvation to everyone who believes, to the Jew first and also to the Greek. (Romans 1:16)

Chapter 3 Discussion Questions

1. Why do you suppose we grow spiritually more from "valley days" than "mountaintop moments"?

2. Why do you think the Gospel is actually quite simple while the Christian life can be very difficult to truly live out in any generation?

3. Consider this statement: "God makes it abundantly clear that our lives and callings are just as crucial to our generation on His behalf." Why is this true? Why are we often tempted to shy away from this calling? Discuss.

4. Regarding Hebrews 12:1–3, how does this passage tie us back to our forefathers in the faith? How does it potentially connect us to Christ followers in the future?

5. Discuss Genesis 15:1–7, 13–16, and 18–21, God's Covenant with Abraham, focusing on his belief of what the Lord was telling him.

6. Regarding Hebrews 13:7–9, how does the statement "Jesus Christ is the same yesterday and today and forever" encourage us to stand strong on God's truth in our everyday lives?

7. Consider Egyptologist David Rohl's comment, "As an agnostic, I don't need these stories to be true." How might his candor and lack of fear toward his own convictions challenge and inspire us in our beliefs?

8. How might Rohl's obvious knowledge of Scripture and background of the Old Testament's key people motivate us in our own biblical knowledge and insight?

9. How does the Gospel of Jesus fit into this big story from Adam to Moses to the Prophets to Paul?

10. Regarding the Gospel presentation from Romans, would anyone like to share your own conversion story or how one of these verses impacted your decision for Christ?

Notes:

....

....

....

....

....

....

....

....

....

....

 CHAPTER 4

The Turning of the Tables

Chance is perhaps the pseudonym of God when he does not want to sign.
— *Theophile Gautier* [6]

With a fresh outlook and a new direction, I decided to hit the reset button on my investigation back at the first step—the Arrival of the Israelites in Egypt. Rohl's interview had focused on Joseph, so that was where I would begin again.

As is normal fare with God, the first step of building this new nation was not a grand or even conventional entrance for His people. The first descendant of God's Covenant partner to arrive in Egypt was through one man. Just as Adam was the first to populate Earth, Joseph was the lone candidate to begin the fulfillment of God's plan for Israel. But delivering divine destiny was not at all what this young man was thinking as his journey began.

Jacob lived in the land of his father's sojournings, in the land of Canaan. These are the generations of Jacob. Joseph, being seventeen years old, was pasturing the flock with his brothers. He was a boy with the sons of Bilhah and Zilpah, his father's wives. And Joseph brought a bad report of them to their father. Now Israel loved Joseph more than any other of his sons, because he was the son of his old age. And he made him a robe of many colors. But when his brothers saw that their father loved him more than all his brothers, they hated him and could not speak peacefully to him. (Genesis 37:1–4)

While the recipe for trouble brewing here is obvious, things only get worse. Joseph has two symbolic dreams where all his brothers bowed down to him, and he tells the entire family about them. Imagine for a moment the youngest and favored child in a large family proclaiming that one day they will all kneel before him. What were actually prophetic dreams became weapons in his brothers' hands. The jealousy and hatred grew deeper. They were all away caring for the family's sheep herds when their father told Joseph to go check on them and report back.

They saw him from afar, and before he came near to them they conspired against him to kill him. They said to one another, "Here comes this dreamer. Come now, let us kill him and throw him into one of the pits. Then we will say that a fierce animal has devoured him, and we will see what will become of his dreams." But when Reuben heard it, he rescued him out of their hands, saying, "Let us not take his life." And Reuben said to them, "Shed no blood; throw him into this pit here in the wilderness, but do not lay a hand on him"—that he might rescue him out of their hand to restore him to his father. So when Joseph came to his brothers, they stripped him of his robe, the robe of many colors that he wore. And they took him and threw him into a pit. The pit was empty; there was no water in it. (Genesis 37:18–24)

Soon, a caravan of Ishmaelites came by on their way to … wait for it … Egypt. Judah made the suggestion that they sell him to the traders as a slave. The brothers agreed and a deal was struck. Joseph was pulled up out of the pit and, after what amounts to a human trafficking transaction, was forcibly taken.

Stop and think about Joseph's myriad of emotions as he witnessed his own brothers trade him for twenty shekels of silver. (Ironically, Jesus was sold out for 30 shekels.) Then as the caravan started on its way, not a single one of them took action or tried to stop this from happening. He realized in that moment they really did hate him and did not care if he lived or died. Fear gripped him of where he was going and what would happen to him or be done to him, wherever he was being taken.

In this powerful and dramatic story, we see an amazing amount of family dysfunction. But we have the unique vantage point from God's perspective that He was simultaneously accomplishing His purposes and fulfilling His promise to Abraham. What appears at this point to be only a tragic crime will eventually create a national family with God as the King.

Joseph's enslavement, as well as the time he spent in prison on a false accusation, eventually ended. In God's timing, he was raised up and rewarded by Pharaoh for saving the country of Egypt from the coming famine, to the point where he was made second-in-command of the nation. It was a moving scene when Joseph finally revealed himself to his brothers who had come to Egypt looking for food.

> *Then Joseph could not control himself before all those who stood by him. He cried, "Make everyone go out from me." So no one stayed with him when Joseph made himself known to his brothers. And he wept aloud, so that the Egyptians heard it, and the household of Pharaoh heard it. And Joseph said to his brothers, "I am Joseph! Is my father still alive?" But his brothers could not answer him, for they were dismayed at his presence. So Joseph said to his brothers, "Come near to me, please."*
>
> *And they came near. And he said, "I am your brother, Joseph, whom you sold into Egypt. And now do not be distressed or angry with yourselves because you sold me here, for God sent me before you to preserve life. For the famine has been in the land these two years, and there are yet five years in which there will be neither plowing nor harvest. And God sent me before you to preserve for you a remnant on earth, and to keep alive for you many survivors. So it was not you who sent me here, but God. He has made me a father to Pharaoh, and lord of all his house and ruler over all the land of Egypt.*
>
> *Hurry and go up to my father and say to him, 'Thus says your son Joseph, God has made me lord of all Egypt. Come down to me; do not tarry. You shall dwell in the land of Goshen, and you shall be near me, you and your children and your children's children, and your flocks, your herds, and all that you have." (Genesis 45: 1-10)*

Later in life, Joseph, speaking to his family, made a single powerful statement to make sense of his fateful journey:

"As for you, you meant evil against me, but God meant it for good."
(Genesis 50:20)

This is a powerful reminder to us all that when life appears to be literally falling down around us, God is building something "far more abundantly than all that we ask or think" (Ephesians 3:20). That which has been invisible to human eyes is finally revealed to be for our best when all the pieces are in place.

Let me give you a little more background into my own valley of despair. I had pitched the Exodus film as a one-year project, but after the first year I was nowhere near completion. One Sunday morning in a quiet moment before church started, I was sitting in the pew and asked God to forgive me for not finishing the project on time. In a flash, a strong thought swept through my mind: "It's done when I say it's done, not when you're tired of working on it." From that moment clarity came for me, and I knew I had to take the time to get the film right. This was God's project, not mine. I was simply a steward.

It seemed there were two seasons. One was exciting yet intimidating as the investigation kept expanding into new areas beyond its original scope. The other was when there would be long stretches of no activity as we tried to determine the next step or wait for further funding. It was during one of these wilderness periods that I became very discouraged; you might even call it depression. This happened four or five years into the production, and I ended up buying a camping trailer and in the course of a year camped over ninety days. I just needed time alone staring into the campfire, wondering if and how the project would ever come together.

So many times, once I was farther down the road in my own journey, I could see how God had worked on my behalf to lead me to a new discovery, orchestrate an interview, initiate an encounter, or even providentially protect our team as we were often in such violent places. When we are walking in the dark, we must remind ourselves that God will not always bring the light when we want, but always just in time to see that He has been there all along.

And I will lead the blind in a way that they do not know, in paths that they have not known I will guide them. I will turn the darkness before them into light, the rough places into level ground. These are the things I do, and I do not forsake them. (Isaiah 42:16)

Three Percent in Thirty Years

I learned of another Egyptologist who paralleled Rohl's conclusion regarding the dig at Avaris, so I made arrangements to visit him. I sat down with Professor Charles Aling from the University of Northwestern in St. Paul, not far from my home, with the camera rolling.

The conversation quickly turned to my now much-discussed on-site encounter with Manfred Bietak. Aling informed me that in thirty years of excavation, Bietak's team had only unearthed about 3 percent of what is believed to be in the ground at Avaris. The professor added, "So when people say, 'Oh, there's nothing that's been found to verify the Bible' and so on, they're basing it on awfully slim evidence."

Funny how a scientist or scholar's assertion can make a 3 percent discovery sound like a 100 percent declaration! Here was yet another lesson to be learned in assumption, solely from this one comment from Professor Aling.

So I began my questions regarding Rohl's detailed information about Avaris: "Would it be unusual for a tomb to have a statue?"

Aling answered, "No. It's unusual to have one this large. This would probably be twice the size of a normal human being."

I continued, "What does that tell you when the statue's larger?"

"That it's a very important person," he answered. "Now, of course this is not a pharaoh's tomb or a palace, but the man who lived there, you can identify his nationality by looking at the fragments of the statue. These reveal three things: the hairstyle he had, his weapon—a throw stick, and then the coloration of the skin. The skin is yellow. All those things indicate that this would have been a Syro-Palestinian."

So, point-blank, I asked, "Do you think this is Joseph?"

Aling answered in cautious archaeological style, "Either it is Joseph, or its somebody who had a career remarkably the same as Joseph did. It's just an incredible thing to find this at this time period."

I want to pause and insert a reminder here that, early on, I had an overwhelming amount of information and opinions piling up against the Bible's timeline. Had my frustration and discouragement brought me to the point of quitting, not only would I not have met and spoken with Rohl, but I certainly wouldn't have met and had an interview with Aling.

Sitting there in that moment, hearing the tables continue to turn, brought proof that had I stopped short, I might have come to the personal crisis of losing faith or decided for myself that the Bible is not true at all. We see throughout the whole of Scripture how vital perseverance is to our journey through life and our walk with God. I certainly experienced this reality of faith firsthand. My goal in sharing this is not to pat myself on the back, but to point out how critical one-step-at-a-time obedience is to all of us in becoming who we are meant to be.

James the brother of Jesus is believed by most scholars to be the writer of the New Testament book of the same name. He, like Joseph's brothers, would have had plenty of reason to be jealous of the attention given to another family member. But listen to his words, written after Jesus' Crucifixion and Resurrection, in regards to pushing through when the days are long and the odds overwhelming:

> Count it all joy, my brothers, when you meet trials of various kinds, for you know that the testing of your faith produces steadfastness. And let steadfastness have its full effect, that you may be perfect and complete, lacking in nothing. ... Blessed is the man who remains steadfast under trial, for when he has stood the test he will receive the crown of life, which God has promised to those who love him. ... But be doers of the word, and not hearers only, deceiving yourselves. For if anyone is a hearer of the word and not a doer, he is like a man who looks intently at his natural face in a mirror. For he looks at himself and goes away and at once forgets what he was like. But the one who looks into the perfect law, the law of liberty,

and perseveres, being no hearer who forgets but a doer who acts, he will be blessed in his doing. (James 1:2–4, 12, 22–25)

Living in a culture where the path of least resistance has increasingly become the norm, may we all remind ourselves of the biblical gift of perseverance to one day "be perfect and complete."

From Slave to Success

Regarding the impact and effects of unflinching obedience, I must point out a pattern of evidence that is crucial to Joseph's life story.

The Lord was with Joseph, and he became a successful man. (Genesis 39:2)

But the Lord was with Joseph and showed him steadfast love and gave him favor. (Genesis 39:21)

"Since God has shown you all this, there is none so discerning and wise as you are. You shall be over my house, and all my people shall order themselves as you command." (Genesis 41:39–40)

So it was not you who sent me here, but God. He has made me a father to Pharaoh, and lord of all his house and ruler over all the land of Egypt. (Genesis 45:8)

Success. Favor. Authority. Obedience to God and the resulting blessing was a common theme throughout Joseph's life. There is an undeniable biblical connection between faith and works, obedience and blessing. We see time and time again throughout Scripture how God will take even a small portion of submission to Him and turn it into a miraculous moment. Abraham's Covenant Partner, God, had planted, grown, and harvested a bumper crop of fruit in Joseph's life that people, even the pharaoh, could "taste and see that the Lord is good" (Psalm 34:8). Such is the result of obedience.

Let's return to Joseph and watch the highlight reel that took him from slave to second-in-command of Egypt.

- The traders sold Joseph to Potiphar, Pharaoh's captain of the guard (Genesis 37:36).
- Potiphar placed Joseph in charge of his entire household (Genesis 39:4).
- Potiphar's wife tried to seduce Joseph, but when he refused, she accused him of attempted rape (Genesis 39:11–18).
- Potiphar placed Joseph in prison (Genesis 39:20).
- The warden put Joseph in charge of all the prisoners (Genesis 39:22).
- Joseph interpreted the dreams of two of Pharaoh's employees who were in prison (Genesis 40:5–19).
- Pharaoh had strange dreams that he wanted interpreted, and the employee recalled Joseph (Genesis 41:1–13).
- Pharaoh sends for Joseph, and he not only interprets the dreams but also offers a plan for the nation to avoid a famine and give prosperity to the throne (Genesis 41:14–36).
- Pharaoh places Joseph over the entire nation, second only to him (Genesis 41:37–43).
- Joseph forgives his brothers and invites his entire family to live in Egypt (Genesis 45:1-10).

Joseph was thirty years old when he entered the service of Pharaoh king of Egypt. And Joseph went out from the presence of Pharaoh and went through all the land of Egypt. During the seven plentiful years the earth produced abundantly, and he gathered up all the food of these seven years, which occurred in the land of Egypt, and put the food in the cities. He put in every city the food from the fields around it. And Joseph stored up grain in great abundance, like the sand of the sea, until he ceased to measure it, for it could not be measured. (Genesis 41:46–49)

The thread of continuity throughout the Bible is always intriguing. Here, the writer uses the same analogy of the infinite amount of sand on the beach, drawing back to God's Covenant language with Abraham to "make your off-spring as the sand of the sea, which cannot be numbered" (Genesis 32:12).

David Rohl had made a fascinating connection regarding Joseph, the Pharaoh's dreams, and the Nile River. He shared, "There is a canal or water-way that connects the Nile to the Fayum Basin, a large lake area, which has the name Bahr Yusef, which means the 'waterway of Joseph.' I think [Joseph] made it. I think it was under his instructions as vizier of Egypt that the canal was cut. And it was cut to divert half the water from the Nile into the Fayum Basin. You then get back to the situation where the water levels are just right for growing crops. It's still in use today, and the construction of this water diversion system is dated to the same period as the early settlement of Avaris."

I recalled the biblical story of the seven years of famine occurring after the seven years of plenty, which caused me to wonder if there was ever a time in Egyptian history when a dramatic shift of wealth and power occurred between the people of Egypt and the pharaoh.

The next link in my new chain of events was an interview with Dr. Bryant Wood at his home in Pennsylvania. Now Research Director for the Associates for Biblical Research, Wood is an archaeologist who is known for his years of studying the Exodus and the Conquest.

What on Earth Happened?

As we sat down and I asked Wood about the seven years of plenty that Joseph directed, he told me something surprising: "Well, if you examine Joseph's famine policy, you'll see he was very astute. He didn't simply give the grain away, as some kind of giant welfare program. He sold the grain, and so the people had to buy the grain. So over those seven years, all the wealth of Egypt came into Joseph, which meant that it came to Pharaoh, because Joseph was sort of the chief steward, you might say, for Pharaoh."

I then asked, "Do you see anything similar in Egyptian history?"

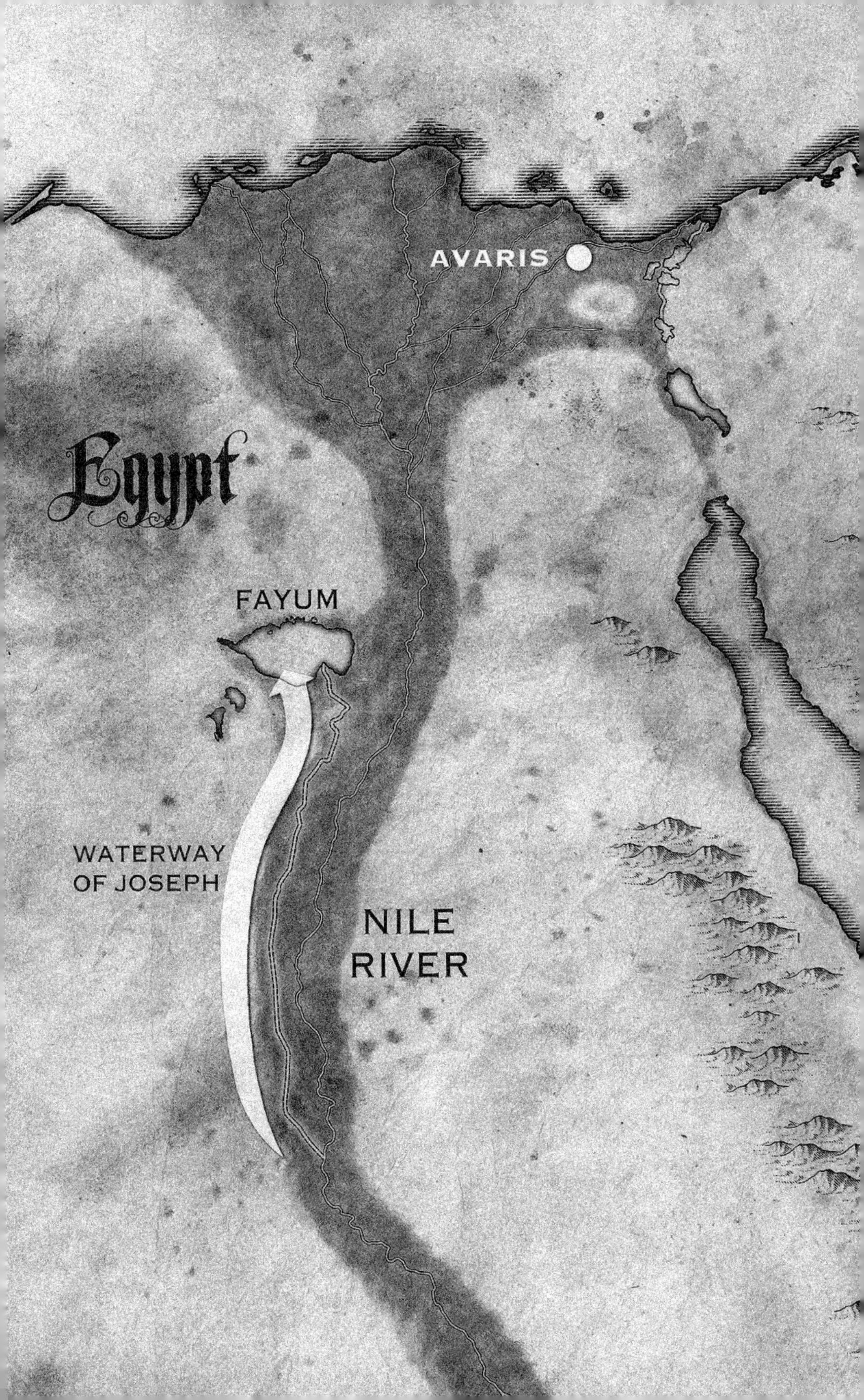
AVARIS
Egypt
FAYUM
WATERWAY
OF JOSEPH
NILE
RIVER

Wood continued, "When we look at Egyptian history, we find something very significant happening at this exact time. Egypt was divided up into areas called nomes, kind of like districts, all over the country. Prior to the time of Joseph, the leaders of these nomes—nomarchs, as they were called—had tremendous wealth and power. We get to a point in Egyptian history when suddenly that all changes and all the wealth is concentrated with the pharaoh. What on earth happened here? If you read the Egyptian history books, there is no explanation for it. They don't know what happened or how it happened. I mean this was a tremendous socio-economic change in Egypt, a very conservative country, which does not change easily, but suddenly the whole thing is turned upside down. Instead of the nomarchs having all this power and authority and wealth, it's all concentrated with the pharaoh."

"So what do you think happened?" I asked.

"Well, we have the answer in the Bible, and it's Joseph's famine policy, and he brings the wealth into Pharaoh ... and it fits exactly with Egyptian history."

Connected to this, Rohl had mentioned another detail that matched the occurrence of famine and central control at this time in Egypt. He had previously told me, "We have this new administration that sets up in Egypt, an agency called the Department of the People's Giving, where the people grow their crops and bring them to government storehouses where they're kept, and then, apparently, in times of crisis, the food's then redistributed back to the people. This Department of the People's Giving exactly fits the Joseph story."

Rohl believed these two events—the years of plenty and the years of famine—occurred during the reign of two Middle Kingdom pharaohs—Senusret III and his son Amenemhat III. Rohl states, "I believe that Amenemhat was Joseph's Pharaoh. His statue is depicted with worry lines. His ears are turned out so that he can listen to the concerns of the people. I think this is an indication that in his time Egypt was experiencing serious problems. And guess what? ... Amenemhat builds his pyramid right next to Bahr Yusef, the Waterway of Joseph."

At this pyramid tomb of Avaris, we find an incredible match of archaeological evidence to biblical text.

So Joseph remained in Egypt, he and his father's house. Joseph lived 110 years. And Joseph saw Ephraim's children of the third generation. The children also of Machir the son of Manasseh were counted as Joseph's own. And Joseph said to his brothers, "I am about to die, but God will visit you and bring you up out of this land to the land that he swore to Abraham, to Isaac, and to Jacob." Then Joseph made the sons of Israel swear, saying, "God will surely visit you, and you shall carry up my bones from here." So Joseph died, being 110 years old. They embalmed him, and he was put in a coffin in Egypt. (Genesis 50:22–26)

Rohl delivers this knockout punch: "What matches the story even more incredibly is that this pyramid tomb was empty when the archaeologists found it. There was nothing in it at all apart from a few fragments of this smashed statue. There were no bones, no mummy beads, no coffin wood, nothing. It was cleaned out."

To sweep aside what anyone might surmise, I asked, "So it was a grave robber?"

Rohl quickly asserted, "What grave robber is going to take the bones? Only people who are treating the body with reverence take the bones. The body was taken out and all the grave goods were taken out. I think this is the tomb of Joseph, the pyramid tomb of Joseph, honored by Pharaoh with a colossal statue, and that when Moses decided to take the people out of Egypt, he made sure he fulfilled that promise to Joseph to take the body out of the tomb and take it to Shechem and bury him in the Promised Land."

Joseph, God's first man in Egypt, comes full circle with his remains being transplanted in Canaan—the Promised Land. This amazing revelation for me—and turn of events for the film—were brought to my attention not by biblical scholars or theologians but by Egyptologists and archaeologists. The same type of scientists that had told me early on that this path would lead nowhere!

Random Chance, Righteous Choice

Hearing all of this converging research and intersecting information from Aling, Wood, and Rohl made me take a step back and ask, "While unlikely, could this all be a coincidence?"

But what about coincidence? Luck? Chance? What do we do with these concepts in life? Circumstances coming from seemingly different directions, appearing to line up, yet meeting at a single crossroads? Where do these come from? How did this thought of randomness pervade our thinking?

As so often we have seen, we need to go back to the beginning—or better said, what you believe the beginning to be. Earlier, we touched on origin belief—how we began—but let's go deeper to consider how we process a matching up of events to a certain conclusion, especially when this has spiritual ramifications.

If someone makes the decision that there is no God involved with how we arrived here, then our origination has to be explained by what many call "random chance." We "just happened." Life "found a way." The right combination of material, be it primordial slime or "non-living matter," came into being and diversified to become "living matter," and the evolutionary chain was set into motion. If the progression of protozoa to amphibians to apes to humans is our belief, we then simultaneously create a world full of coincidence. If we "just happened," then life ongoing must continue to "just happen."

Webster defines luck as "a force that brings good fortune or adversity," referencing that it can be good or bad. The secondary definition is "the events or circumstances that operate for or against an individual."[7] Now let's look at some opposite concepts: intentional, planned, and providence.

Even the very definition of luck begins with the words force and event. We have enough sense and logic to know, regardless of how we believe, that any origin must start somewhere with something! If you and I are indeed intentional creations, planned beings, and providential people, then our lives cannot be filled with random chance. Every day has a plan. Every plan has a purpose. Every purpose is part of God's provision.

Just like Joseph, our lives have so many tragic moments when we feel betrayed, rejected, accused, and forgotten, but then those make us stronger for the moments when we are favored, promoted, and blessed. God uses all of these to remind us that we are very much alive and living in His intentional world.

Does this possible origin create a much better outlook and self-image of who we are? Consider the psalmist's belief:

O Lord, you have searched me and known me! You know when I sit down and when I rise up; you discern my thoughts from afar. You search out my path and my lying down and are acquainted with all my ways. Even before a word is on my tongue, behold, O Lord, you know it altogether. You hem me in, behind and before, and lay your hand upon me. ... For you formed my inward parts; you knitted me together in my mother's womb. I praise you, for I am fearfully and wonderfully made. Wonderful are your works; my soul knows it very well. My frame was not hidden from you, when I was being made in secret, intricately woven in the depths of the earth. Your eyes saw my unformed substance; in your book were written, every one of them, the days that were formed for me, when as yet there was none of them. (Psalm 139:1–5, 13–16)

And then, there it is again, from Abraham's descendants to Joseph's overflowing grain to God's love for us: His involvement in the most minute details of our lives turn the tables on the world and shows us who we truly are.

 How precious to me are your thoughts, O God! How vast is the sum of them! If I would count them, they are more than the sand. (Psalm 139:17–18)

Chapter 4 Discussion Questions

1. Why do you suppose we see so often, as in the case of Joseph, how God's ways are so different from what and how we would write the story?

2. What can we glean for our own life circumstances after viewing Joseph's story from God's perspective?

3. Consider Tim's statement: "When we are walking in the dark, we must remind ourselves that God will not always bring the light when we want, but always just in time to see that He has been there all along." Would anyone like to share a testimony of when you had this experience?

4. Consider Tim's statement from Aling's information: "Funny how a scientist or scholar's assertion can make a 3 percent discovery sound like a 100 percent declaration!" Why do we accept expert opinions so easily with little examination?

5. Discuss the archaeological information about Joseph's tomb.

6. From the list of Scriptures about Joseph, discuss God's constant interaction with his life through good and bad circumstances.

7. Discuss Rohl's and Wood's dialogues about Joseph's preparation for the famine.

8. Discuss Rohl's dialogue and connection to Genesis 50:22–26 regarding Joseph's tomb.

9. Talk about the concepts of coincidence and random chance versus God's intentionality and planning.

10. Why does your origin belief have so much impact on how you live your life?

Notes:

....

....

....

....

....

....

....

....

....

....

....

....

....

 CHAPTER 5

Shekels & Shackles

Never be afraid to trust an unknown future to a known God.
— Corrie ten Boom [8]

Throughout the history of the world, we find countless small settlements that went through a sudden expansion of growth to eventually become significant cities. My own hometown, where I still live today, has this as its story.

My birthplace and stomping grounds was originally across the river and a few miles from a rough frontier trading post located along the east bank of the Mississippi River called "Pig's Eye." In 1841, a Catholic priest, Father Lucien Galtier, settled there and built a small chapel. According to local legend, Galtier once publicly declared, "Pig's Eye! Converted thou shalt be like Saul. Arise, and be, henceforth, Saint Paul!"

The priest was making an obvious reference to Saul of Tarsus' dramatic conversion into whom God renamed as Paul, the church planter and Scripture writer, adding the "Saint" from his Catholic recognition. The tiny community that began as Pig's Eye, through migration and multiplication, lived up to Galtier's promotion and eventually grew into the great city that became the capital of Minnesota: St. Paul.

This same concept of rapid and expansive growth—Multiplication—was the second stage on the Wall of Time. This was an era when God grew the Israelites' displaced nation in virtually every way.

These are the names of the sons of Israel who came to Egypt with Jacob, each with his household: Reuben, Simeon, Levi, and Judah, Issachar, Zebulun, and Benjamin, Dan and Naphtali, Gad and Asher. All the descendants of Jacob were seventy persons; Joseph was already in Egypt. Then Joseph died, and all his brothers and all that generation. But the people of Israel were fruitful and increased greatly; they multiplied and grew exceedingly strong, so that the land was filled with them. (Exodus 1:1–7)

The Israelites, God's people:
- Grew in number
- Gained strength
- Filled the new land

We must constantly remind ourselves that God began this incredible work with one solitary man, brought as a slave, after having been rejected and abandoned by his own brothers. An act of tragic jealousy and hatred gave birth to the blessing of an entire nation. This is a testimony to the realities of God's capabilities.

Let us also not forget that this same God is alive in your own soul—or available to live in your soul—and can take the heartbreaks, rejections, abandonments, and tragedies of your life and turn them into blessings, strength, and fullness. This concept of multiplication can happen inside you as God matures and nurtures you to be all He designed you to be. His precepts and principles are just as fit for individuals as nations, for His truth is timeless and limitless.

He has shown his people the power of his works, in giving them the inheritance of the nations. The works of his hands are faithful and just; all his precepts are trustworthy; they are established forever and ever, to be performed with faithfulness and uprightness. He sent redemption to his people; he has commanded his covenant forever. Holy and awesome is his name! (Psalm 111:6–9)

City of Foreigners

In one of my interviews with Rohl, I asked him about this stage in Israel's history and the discovery of Semitic expansion at Avaris: "David, what happened next in the Delta that matches the biblical story?"

He answered, "At first there is a virgin land with no population at all. And suddenly there is a small group of Semitic people settled there. There's probably a dozen or fifteen houses, let's say about seventy or one hundred people all told. And over a period of maybe three or four generations, it becomes a very large city, one of the largest cities in the ancient world."

I continued, "What's unique about it?"

Rohl explained, "This is a city of foreigners in the Egyptian Delta, and it's been allowed by the Egyptian state. These Semitic peoples have migrated here, bringing their flocks with them, and are living here and surviving in such a way that they became quite rich and wealthy."

In my interview with Professor James Hoffmeier, I inquired about this same topic, "What does the archaeology say about the area Joseph's family is said to have settled?"

Hoffmeier stated, "We do know that there was a large Semitic-speaking population, which probably came in from Syria, Canaan, sometime in the early part of the second millennium BC. Their remains have been found at a number of sites. We have tombs that are clearly those of foreigners—Semites. We can tell this by the pottery and the kind of weapons. These are not Egyptian-type axes and daggers. In some cases, they have donkeys buried with them. This was not an Egyptian practice. So the types of tombs, the types of architecture, are not Egyptian. These are clearly foreigners who have moved into Egypt and have lived there long enough to establish mudbrick homes and some sort of permanent dwellings."

Hoffmeier also told me about a magnificent tomb built by Khnumhotep at the site of Beni Hasan in central Egypt. On its walls was found a painting depicting a caravan of thirty-seven Semitic traders who had come to Egypt with their families. The tomb of Khnumhotep II is one of the last

examples of the extravagant wealth and power held by the regional nomarchs before their sudden decline and the rise of pharaohs Senusret III and his son Amenemhat III.

Evidence in the Right Time

During the course of my investigation into this stage, I heard about John Bimson, an author and a professor of the Old Testament in Bristol, England. He has written extensively about archaeology and the accounts of the Exodus and the Conquest. I was curious to see what information he might have about this multiplication in the Delta area of Egypt. Fortunately, I was able to arrange an interview while in England.

I asked Professor Bimson, "What connections have you identified between the biblical account and the growth of the Semitic site of Avaris in the Nile Delta?"

He smiled as he answered with a question, "Well, did you know there are more sites than just Avaris with a Semitic population?"

"Really?" I was surprised by his response and continued, "How many sites would there have been?"

Bimson replied, "If we go back to the 18th and 19th centuries BC, you've got a good many settlements, twenty or more, which would fit the land of Goshen where the Bible says the Israelites were settled. Many of these have not been fully excavated yet."

"How do they compare to Avaris?" I asked.

The scholar went on, "We don't know whether they're as big as the Avaris site until people start digging there—no one knew how big that was until excavation began. So there could be a lot of stuff in the ground waiting to be discovered and to throw a lot more light on this period of Asiatic settlement."

Amazed, I asked, "Do you think these sites could possibly represent the early Israelites' population growth in the Delta?"

Matter-of-factly, Bimson stated, "Until we have more excavations of more of these sites, we can't say exactly when or why they arrived or exactly why or when they left. But there's certainly plenty of evidence for Asiatic—that is,

Semitic—settlement in that area in Egypt at a time that would fit the biblical accounts of Joseph and the arrival of the tribes leading up to the Exodus."

So I asked, "In your opinion, does the archaeology in the Delta reflect what the Bible says happened?"

He responded, "It fits the archaeology if you look for the archaeological evidence in the right time period."

"In the right time period"—there was the potential answer yet again, shared by a different expert. You'll recall from our past discussions that the Egyptologists who disagree with these interpretations and believe these Semitic settlements were too early to be linked to the Israelites are assuming the Exodus happened at the time of Ramesses—while in the earlier period around the Middle Kingdom, archaeology does show massive numbers of Semites living in ancient Egypt. This continued the controversy, but my own "excavating" research was paying off.

What Does This Mean?

The multiplication of the Israelites in Egypt is like a foreshadowing of another great time of rapid expansion—that of the early Church—but of a different nature: growth in the spiritual realm, not the physical.

After Jesus' Resurrection and Ascension, He had told the disciples to wait in Jerusalem. Then, unannounced, the promised Holy Spirit showed up and filled the obedient followers. What happened next is the greatest—and fastest—revival in the history of mankind.

Now there were dwelling in Jerusalem Jews, devout men from every nation under heaven. And at this sound the multitude came together, and they were bewildered, because each one was hearing them speak in his own language. And they were amazed and astonished, saying, "Are not all these who are speaking Galileans? And how is it that we hear, each of us in his own native language? Parthians and Medes and Elamites and residents of Mesopotamia, Judea and Cappadocia, Pontus and Asia, Phrygia and Pamphylia, Egypt and the parts of Libya belonging to Cyrene, and visitors from Rome, both Jews and proselytes, Cretans and Arabians—we hear them telling in our own tongues the mighty works of God." And all were amazed and perplexed, saying to one another, "What does this mean?"... But Peter, standing with the eleven, lifted up his voice and addressed them: "Men of Judea and all who dwell in Jerusalem, let this be known to you, and give ear to my words. ... But this is what was uttered through the prophet Joel: "'And in the last days it shall be, God declares, that I will pour out my Spirit on all flesh, and your sons and your daughters shall prophesy, and your young men shall see visions, and your old men shall dream dreams; even on my male servants and female servants in those days I will pour out my Spirit, and they shall prophesy. And I will show wonders in the heavens above and signs on the earth below, blood, and fire, and vapor of smoke; the sun shall be turned to darkness and the moon to blood, before the day of the Lord comes, the great and magnificent day. And it shall come to pass that everyone who calls upon the name of the Lord shall be saved.' (Acts 2:5–14, 16–21)

Once again, we see how critical the historical events of the Old Testament are to the birth of Christianity. Peter used the words of the prophet Joel, who all these people would have known well, to bridge to the truth about Jesus.

"Men of Israel, hear these words: Jesus of Nazareth, a man attested to you by God with mighty works and wonders and signs that God did through him in your midst, as you yourselves know—this Jesus, delivered up according to the definite plan and foreknowledge of God, you crucified and killed by the hands of lawless men. God raised him up, loosing the pangs of death, because it was not possible for him to be held by it. For David says concerning him, 'I saw the Lord always before me, for he is at my right hand that I may not be shaken; therefore my heart was glad, and my tongue rejoiced; my flesh also will dwell in hope. For you will not abandon my soul to Hades, or let your Holy One see corruption. You have made known to me the paths of life; you will make me full of gladness with your presence.' Brothers, I may say to you with confidence about the patriarch David that he both died and was buried, and his tomb is with us to this day. Being therefore

a prophet, and knowing that God had sworn with an oath to him that he would set one of his descendants on his throne, he foresaw and spoke about the resurrection of the Christ, that he was not abandoned to Hades, nor did his flesh see corruption. This Jesus God raised up, and of that we all are witnesses. Being therefore exalted at the right hand of God, and having received from the Father the promise of the Holy Spirit, he has poured out this that you yourselves are seeing and hearing. For David did not ascend into the heavens, but he himself says, 'The Lord said to my Lord, sit at my right hand, until I make your enemies your footstool.' Let all the house of Israel therefore know for certain that God has made him both Lord and Christ, this Jesus whom you crucified." (Acts 2:22–36)

The Holy Spirit empowered Peter to use David's own words and lineage, also quickly recognized by all those who were listening, to create yet another historical connection to the reality of who Jesus was and is.

There is great authority spoken in Peter's message, not just to the Jewish people gathered that day, but to all who would read these words in future generations as he called out, "Let all the house of Israel therefore know …"

So what was the people's response? After all, so many times Moses, Joshua, and the Prophets preached amazing messages only to be met with ridicule, threats, and near riots.

Now when they heard this they were cut to the heart, and said to Peter and the rest of the apostles, "Brothers, what shall we do?" And Peter said to them, "Repent and be baptized every one of you in the name of Jesus Christ for the forgiveness of your sins, and you will receive the gift of the Holy Spirit. For the promise is for you and for your children and for all who are far off, everyone whom the Lord our God calls to himself." And with many other words he bore witness and continued to exhort them, saying, "Save yourselves from this crooked generation." So those who received his word were baptized, and there were added that day about three thousand souls. (Acts 2:37–41)

We must not miss two important components of their response. First, the word *brothers* indicates they recognize this message is from their own people. And, second, they were accepting the truth shared and wanted to know what action to now take—"what shall we do?"

We know from both historians and theologians that in the days of the Bible only men were counted; therefore, the three thousand meant only the males who responded. Potentially, the number of people and households represented could have been many thousands more. And remember, all these people who had come to Jerusalem for the Feast of Pentecost would be traveling home soon, taking this new Gospel with them back to their home countries. God's *multiplication* plan for His Son's sacrificial work on the cross was now fully engaged by the Holy Spirit and about to spread throughout the known world.

This concept of Multiplication—physically and spiritually—in Exodus and Acts displays the power of God at work in His people. Yet another pattern of evidence seen from His hand.

Too Many & Too Mighty

The next step on the Wall of Time was Slavery.

For those new to this story or seeing it with fresh eyes, the leap from prosperity to slavery seems to be an odd turn of events, from such thriving expansion to imposed bondage. That's quite a plot twist. Here's what happened …

Now there arose a new king over Egypt, who did not know Joseph. And he said to his people, "Behold, the people of Israel are too many and too mighty for us. Come, let us deal shrewdly with them, lest they multiply, and, if war breaks out, they join our enemies and fight against us and escape from the land." Therefore they set taskmasters over them to afflict them with heavy burdens. They built for Pharaoh store cities, Pithom and Raamses. But the more they were oppressed, the more they multiplied and the more they spread abroad. And the Egyptians were in dread of the people of Israel. So they ruthlessly made the people of Israel work as slaves and made their lives bitter with hard service, in mortar and brick, and in all kinds of work in the field. In all their work they ruthlessly made them work as slaves. (Exodus 1:8–14)

Did you recognize our key verse (v. 11) from an earlier chapter—the Raamses (Ramesses) reference? Now in the context of history, we see that a new pharaoh coming into power became fearful and intimidated by the Israelites, so he decided to implement the ultimate human control—slavery.

Professor Hoffmeier spoke about this connection of slavery to both archaeology and Scripture: "Exodus 1:14 actually says they worked in brick and mortar and agriculture. We have agricultural scenes, especially work in vineyards, where the workers again are Semites, Nubians, and so on. So interestingly, the very two areas the Bible says the Israelites were forced to work in—agriculture and construction—are the very two places we see this sort of work going on in private tombs in Egypt in the 15th century BC."

I asked David Rohl if the Middle Kingdom had any evidence of slavery at Avaris, to which he responded, "We've got a situation of prosperity followed by a lack of prosperity and a shortage of life. We begin to see in the graves of these people Harris lines in the bones, which indicate shortage of food and nutrients. These people suddenly have become impoverished, and they are dying at an age typically between thirty-two and thirty-four years."

I urged, "What would explain this dramatic change?"

His face somber, Rohl stated, "The obvious answer is slavery."

Pharaoh's fear and concerns over the Israelite population outgrowing and outnumbering his own people escalated. A horribly tragic and evil turn in the story occurred next. The Bible encapsulates this terror into a single verse:

Then Pharaoh commanded all his people, "Every son that is born to the Hebrews you shall cast into the Nile, but you shall let every daughter live." (Exodus 1:22)

There are times throughout human history when we get a glimpse of the stark reality of God's enemy, Satan, and the level of his hatred for God and His children. This event is certainly one, and would not be a quick death by the sword but rather an agonizing death by drowning.

Imagine being a Hebrew mother in the ninth month. Suddenly, your water breaks and the contractions begin. The calling for a midwife and the commotion going on at the house alert the Egyptian soldiers assigned nearby. Just after the baby is born, as the parents are rejoicing and the midwife is wiping away the mucus and cutting the cord, the door flies open. Two soldiers go straight for the baby.

Seeing he is a boy, one grabs the child while the other draws his sword to warn the parents and extended family against retaliation. The soldiers leave the home, as the cries of the mother rise up over the sounds of the city. The soldiers go straight to the Nile's edge, and with all their might toss the newborn far out into the water. This was the terroristic reality these families endured and as despicable of an event as evil could ever imagine. And this travesty would have occurred many times every day.

For the new pharaoh, this would accomplish four things:
- Decrease the Jewish male population
- Discourage Jewish women from getting pregnant
- Limit or eliminate future Jewish leaders from rising into power
- Enact fear and enforce control

As I worked through these biblical accounts, I had to stop at every new juncture and seek out what evidence was available for a particular stage. Again I turned to Rohl, asking, "Is there anything in the archaeology at Avaris that might reflect the death of Israelite infants from this part of the slavery story?"

"At this particular point," he said, "we start to see an increase in the number of infant burials at the site. Now normally in a typical Middle Bronze Age cemetery, we'll get something like 25 percent of burials of infants. In this particular case, it jumps up to an extraordinary figure."

Rohl encouraged me to look into the dig reports from Avaris and what Bietak's team had documented. As I did, I found their record of "an extremely high mortality rate of newborns." According to the report, when all the graves of children aged ten and younger were identified, nearly 50 percent died in the first three months of life!

Because I had to approach all evidence in the mode of an investigative reporter, not jumping to my own conclusions but looking for any and all possibilities, I wondered if this could have been an epidemic that had specifically impacted newborns. But when the graves of adults past this time frame were examined, 60 percent were females, compared to only 40 percent males. The reduction appears to have affected the male population. This massive increase in infant burials at Avaris might certainly be evidence for the genocide of male Israelite children.

This evil tactic was not experienced only at this time; a quite similar event took place just after Jesus' birth by yet another ruthless and fearful ruler:

> *Then Herod, when he saw that he had been tricked by the wise men, became furious, and he sent and killed all the male children in Bethlehem and in all that region who were two years old or under, according to the time that he had ascertained from the wise men. Then was fulfilled what was spoken by the prophet Jeremiah: "A voice was heard in Ramah, weeping and loud lamentation, Rachel weeping for her children; she refused to be comforted, because they are no more." (Matthew 2:16–18)*

Yet again, we see the consistent pattern of the New Testament calling back to the Old. Here, Matthew connects to the prophecy made by Jeremiah, relating to Christ.

Another important detail that joins events such as these atrocities against children is that while the Enemy, Satan, hates all of God's creation, he, lacking omniscience, would not know exactly when Jesus was going to enter reality and history. Once being a resident in Heaven, prior to his mutiny and exile, Satan knew there was a plan to redeem mankind, but he could not know when it was to be engaged. There is most certainly a connection between these infant genocides that involves the great spiritual battle consistently occurring in the heavenly realms.

While our Bibles are divided into books, chapters, and verses, there is a grand unified story of God at work to redeem man to ready for what both the Old and New Testaments refer to as "the new Heaven and new Earth," where evil shall be no more.

Prisoners & Papyrus

Professor James Hoffmeier raised a compelling point to me that he believes brings authenticity to this aspect of the Israelite's story in Egypt. He shared, "Who would invent a story about 'Our ancestors were slaves'? I can see people saying, 'Our ancestors were princes, our ancestors were great merchants, our ancestors were something wonderful and glorious and noble,' but 'We were slaves'? … Why? I mean, if you are going to dream up a story, surely you would come up with a better one than that!"

Compare this to my interview with Mansour Boraik, who told me Egyptian history avoided recorded defeats and that they deemed Pharaoh as the hero of the Exodus. This is quite a contrast to the honest recording of ancestors being driven into slavery.

Another significant piece of evidence I had learned about was regarding an ancient document that was stored in the Brooklyn Museum in New York. This Middle Kingdom Egyptian artifact commonly known as the Brooklyn Papyrus contains a list of slave names that seem to come right out of the early pages of the Bible. Upon contacting the museum, they recommended we purchase their book, which contained a translation and commentary of the papyrus.

In the museum's book, author William C. Hayes associates these Hebrew names with their biblical counterparts, as he wrote regarding the different forms of the name Issachar: "All these names are feminine and cannot be separated from the biblical Hebrew names."

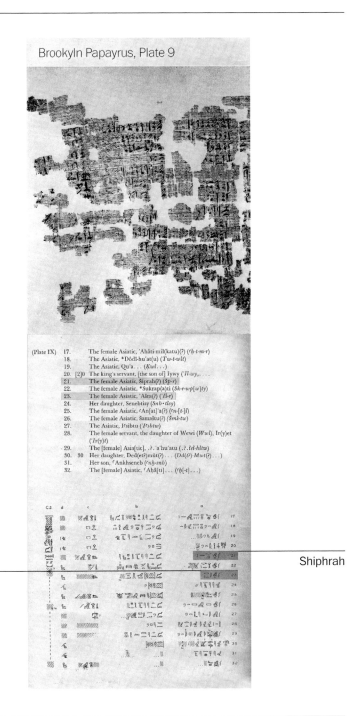

Brookyln Papayrus, Plate 9

(Plate IX) 17. The female Asiatic, 'Ahâti-mil(katu)(?) (*ḥ-t-m-r*)
18. The Asiatic, *Dôdî-hu'at(u) (*Tw-t-wlt*)
19. The Asiatic, Qu'a . . . (*Kwl* . . .)
20. [2]0 The king's servant, [the son of] Iywy ('*Îi-wy, . . .*)
21. The female Asiatic, Šiprah(?) (*Šp-r*)
22. The female Asiatic, *Šukrap(a)ti (*Šk-r-wp[w]ty*)
23. The female Asiatic, 'Aàra(?) ('*Ì-r*)
24. Her daughter, Senebtisy (*Snb·tïsy*)
25. The female Asiatic, ʿAn[at]ʾa(?) (ʿn-[t-]î)
26. The female Asiatic, Šamaštu(?) (*Šmš-tw*)
27. The Asiatic, Iʿsibtu ('*Iʾsibtw*)
28. The female servant, the daughter of Wewi (*Wwî*), Ir(y)et ('*Ir(y)t*)
29. The [female] Asia[tic], .ʔ.'a'hu'atu (.ʔ.*ɪ̀ɪ̀-hltw*)
30. 30 Her daughter, Ded(et?)mût(?) . . . (*Dd(t?)-Mwt(?)* . . .)
31. Her son, ʿAnkhseneb (ʿ*nḫ-snb*)
32. The [female] Asiatic, ʿAḫâ[ti] . . . (ʿ*ḫ[-t]* . . .)

Shiphrah

Asher

David Rohl shared about the Brooklyn Papyrus, "This particular document is quite amazing. It's actually a list—maybe up to a hundred people—of domestic servants from one estate in the south of Egypt. You can imagine that if such a document existed from the north in the Delta, it would be even more spectacular. When we look at these names, 70 percent of them are Semitic names. And some of these names actually occur in the Bible: Issachar and Asher, the names of two of the tribes of Israel, and Shiphrah, one of the Hebrew midwives in the Exodus story. All these names appear in this list of slaves."

Rohl continued, "These are Hebrew, Israelite slaves, and they're in a papyrus from the Thirteenth Dynasty. Not from the Nineteenth Dynasty, not from the time of Ramesses II in the New Kingdom, but from the Thirteenth Dynasty, the Middle Kingdom."

I asked him, "What does this mean to you? What does this say?"

He answered, "This is real evidence for the time when the Israelites were in Egypt as slaves. It's when you get a text, suddenly you've got history. Archaeology you have to interpret. When you have a text, this is something very different."

The Brooklyn Papyrus reveals two other significant connections. First, the slaves from this single estate were predominantly female, matching the excavated grave evidence from Avaris as well as the Bible's account of the genocide of male children. Second, if these were Israelite slaves in the southern sector, the list supports the Bible's account that the Israelite population multiplied and spread throughout Egypt.

As I realized how closely the Brooklyn Papyrus supported the biblical story, I was perplexed, so I asked Rohl, "Why do so many Egyptologists disregard, even ignore, the Brooklyn Papyrus?"

He nodded and said, "Although everybody recognizes that this is a list of Semitic slaves, and everybody recognizes the names appearing in the list are also Israelite names, these can't be the Israelites because it's the wrong time period. The Israelites are much later in history. So these people we're seeing here in this Brooklyn Papyrus cannot be the Israelites."

I pressed, "So *that's* why they disregard it?"

Solemnly frustrated, Rohl answered, "So scholars put the text to one side and say it's another coincidence."

This very human dynamic of brushing aside evidence that might challenge or explain away our chosen paradigm is one of which we must all be cautious. This is exactly what drove me to seek out *patterns* of evidence.

Boldness of Common Men

Earlier, we read the amazing account of the Holy Spirit's coming and Peter's powerful message. By Acts 4, we see Peter and John preaching about Jesus, as verse 4 states, "But many of those who had heard the word believed, and the number of the men came to about five thousand." Thousands were receiving the truth of Jesus. For the religious leaders, this was getting out of hand, just as Pharaoh felt he was losing control of the Israelites.

The Bible says that the high priest and members of the Sadducees had the two disciples arrested. The next day, Peter and John were brought before the council and grilled about their message, specifically about a healing that had taken place. Not surprisingly, their answer turned into more preaching about Jesus, placing the leaders between the proverbial rock and a hard place.

Now when they saw the boldness of Peter and John, and perceived that they were uneducated, common men, they were astonished. And they recognized that they had been with Jesus. But seeing the man who was healed standing beside them, they had nothing to say in opposition. But when they had commanded them to leave the council, they conferred with one another, saying, "What shall we do with these men? For that a notable sign has been performed through them is evident to all the inhabitants of Jerusalem, and we cannot deny it. But in order that it may spread no further among the people, let us warn them to speak no more to anyone in this name." So they called them and charged them not to speak or teach at all in the name of

Jesus. But Peter and John answered them, "Whether it is right in the sight of God to listen to you rather than to God, you must judge, for we cannot but speak of what we have seen and heard." (Acts 4:13–20)

Through my long and difficult journey of linking history to archaeology to Scripture, I certainly relate and resonate with New Testament stories such as this one. I too had to find supernatural boldness at a new level of faith. Compared to these scholars, rabbis, experts, and theologians I interviewed, I too was a "common man" like Peter and John. Many times I felt as if I were standing in front of an opposing council. But even in my days of frustration and doubt, I also now know what it means to decide that I "cannot but speak of what [I] have seen and heard."

By the end of this book, I pray you echo this same statement of experiential belief and also know ...

 "The promise is for you and for your children and for all who are far off, everyone whom the Lord our God calls to himself." (Acts 2:39)

Chapter 5 Discussion Questions

1. Why do you suppose we see so often, as in the case of Joseph, how God's ways are so different from what and how we would write the story?

1. How might this concept of God's Multiplication apply to our lives or seasons of life?

2. Discuss Rohl's, Hoffmeier's, and Bimson's dialogues about Israel's Multiplication.

3. Why do you think archaeologists are so reluctant to match up the Bible to the excavated evidence or consider the possibility that the Exodus happened at an earlier time than they assumed?

4. What are the similarities and differences in Israel's Multiplication and the early Church's rapid expansion?

5. Why would Peter in his first public sermon about Christ have made references regarding the prophet Joel and King David?

6. Discuss Pharaoh's fear of the Israelite's Multiplication. Why might he resort to such horrible tactics?

7. Pharaoh's and Herod's genocide orders were quite similar. Why do you suppose powerful leaders throughout history have launched murderous campaigns against God's people?

8. Discuss Rohl's dialogue and Bietak's archaeology report regarding the infant burials and corresponding decrease in the male population.

9. Discuss the Brooklyn Papyrus and Rohl's dialogue on the scholars' response to the document.

10. Regarding Peter and John's court appearance in Acts 4:13–20, what are some modern-day circumstances where we might be placed in a similar position?

Notes:

....

....

....

....

....

....

....

....

....

 CHAPTER 6

History + Theology = Biography

Moses was the greatest revolutionary of all time.
— *Benjamin Netanyahu, Prime Minister of Israel* [9]

During the time of Pharaoh's genocide of Hebrew male babies, a couple from the Israelite priesthood tribe of Levi had a baby boy. His mother managed to keep him hidden from the authorities for three months. Imagine the stress and fear this new dad and mom must have endured. Even something as normal as a baby crying could be a death sentence.

When the new mother felt she could no longer keep him safely hidden, she did a quite ironic thing. She took her baby boy down to the Nile River. … Wait. What? Had she snapped and decided to inflict the same fate on her son by her own hand as Pharaoh's henchmen would? No, not at all. She placed him carefully in a basket made of bulrushes, the same plant that likely lined the side of the river. She covered the bottom of the basket with bitumen and pitch, effectively creating a tiny camouflaged boat. Then she placed her infant watercraft with its most precious cargo among some reeds at the bank of the river. Whether she knew it or not, this was a divinely inspired plan.

Now, while Scripture does not say this, we are going to make the safe assumption that this loving and ingenious mother prayed one of the strongest and most heartfelt requests of her life. She asked the God of Abraham,

Isaac, and Jacob to keep her child safe and to deliver a first-class miracle for him. The baby boy's older sister decided to do what all great big sisters do and keep watch from a distance, making sure he stayed safe, right in the very place where countless male children had met their end. Such an incredible and ironic scene to unfold.

It "just so happened" that, very soon, Pharaoh's own daughter came down to the Nile to bathe. She spotted the basket and sent a female servant to fetch it from the water for her.

> *When she opened it, she saw the child, and behold, the baby was crying. She took pity on him and said, "This is one of the Hebrews' children." Then his sister said to Pharaoh's daughter, "Shall I go and call you a nurse from the Hebrew women to nurse the child for you?" And Pharaoh's daughter said to her, "Go." So the girl went and called the child's mother. And Pharaoh's daughter said to her, "Take this child away and nurse him for me, and I will give you your wages." So the woman took the child and nursed him."* (Exodus 2:6–9)

Picture this: Who in the known world could have gotten away with this "adoption" of the very type of child Pharaoh had cursed? His daughter, of course. Could she have had "Daddy" wrapped around her little finger? Might he rule a nation with an iron first but melt when he looked into her eyes? I'm betting yes.

The mother placed the baby boy right where other children had been killed. The murderer of Hebrew children, Pharaoh—his own daughter found the boy. The child's big sister, looking on, stepped up and volunteered to find "a Hebrew woman" to breastfeed him. Soon, the mother was again holding her son in her arms, at the command and protection of the royal daughter. Only God could have orchestrated such an event!

And what was the name of this baby who ended up growing into a Hebrew man inside the very house of Pharaoh?

When the child grew older, she brought him to Pharaoh's daughter, and he became her son. She named him Moses, "Because," she said, "I drew him out of the water." (Exodus 2:10)

This Is My Name Forever

The introduction of Moses leads us to the fourth position on the Wall of Time — Judgment.

As an adult, Moses began venturing farther out from the palace grounds, witnessing the horrible conditions under which his own people were living. One day, he came upon an Egyptian relentlessly beating a Hebrew slave. Likely trained in the art of combat, Moses killed the taskmaster and hid his body. Pharaoh found out what had happened and vowed to kill his daughter's adopted son. So Moses decided to run and disappeared into the land of Midian.

And so for the next forty years, he spent his life tending a flock of sheep, wandering in the wilderness. Do you think Moses had regrets? It's safe to say he thought quite a bit about his past and his failure in delivering the people. Do you think he wondered when God was going to act concerning the promises made to Abraham? All of the Israelites knew of the prophecy and longed for deliverance.

I just knew in my heart I was a filmmaker long before I ever got to make a film. I remember the aching inside to create, even though I couldn't articulate it. Most all of us know what it is like to believe we are created to do something, yet it can seem like this will never happen or we decide it never will. This feeling down deep inside causes us to try to solve this great mystery of why we exist.

Yet this discovery can have many layers of meaning and purpose in our lives. After my journey, I am more convinced than ever there is a divine reason for every life.

Several years ago, my wife, Jill, shared a verse with me that became a profound moment in my own journey. Her encouraging words, coupled with

God's Word, gave me a new understanding about the human purpose. The verse was Ephesians 2:10:

For we are His workmanship, created in Christ Jesus for good works, which God prepared beforehand, that we should walk in them.

This was an answer to the deep cry of my soul, the "Why am I here?" In Christ, we are His workmanship created for good works. The truly amazing twist is Paul says that before we were born, these good works were prepared for us. Because God Himself is the Preparer! From this revelatory moment, I began to realize my job was to figure out what those "good works" were in my own life and get busy doing them.

What I've learned about this grand mystery is that some of God's works we are called to do are far beyond our own imagination. We can only accomplish them with divine participation, faith, and courage. Since God has done this for me, I know He can do this for you too. This very point may be exactly why you are reading this book. The answer to your own ache—your own search—may be just around the corner.

Now, back to Moses. God decided to introduce Himself to the fugitive shepherd in a unique yet intriguing way—through a burning, but not consuming, fire in a large desert bush.

Then the Lord said, "I have surely seen the affliction of my people who are in Egypt and have heard their cry because of their taskmasters. I know their sufferings, and I have come down to deliver them out of the hand of the Egyptians and to bring them up out of that land to a good and broad land, a land flowing with milk and honey. ... Come, I will send you to Pharaoh that you may bring my people, the children of Israel, out of Egypt." But Moses said to God, "Who am I that I should go to Pharaoh and bring the children of Israel out of Egypt?" He said, "But I will be with you, and this shall be the sign for you, that I have sent you: when you have brought the people out of Egypt, you shall serve God on this mountain." Then Moses said to God, "If I come to the people of Israel and say to them, 'The God of your fathers has sent me to you,' and they ask me, 'What is his name?' what shall I say to them?" God said to Moses, "I am who I am." And he said, "Say this to the people of Israel, 'I am has sent me to you.'" God also said to Moses, "Say this to the people of Israel: 'The Lord, the God of your fathers, the God of Abraham, the God of Isaac, and the God of Jacob, has sent me to you.' This is my name forever, and thus I am to be remembered throughout all generations." (Exodus 3:7–8, 10–15)

This is a key passage of the Bible, as well as to my focused quest for the patterns of evidence. Here are three points we must be certain to not miss:

- This introduction and interaction between God and Moses is recorded as an actual conversation.

Growing up in Pharaoh's home, Moses would not likely have had the traditional Jewish training and be told the stories of Abraham and his ancestors. But he immediately begins to engage and respond with this Voice coming from the bush as if he quickly put together that this is *that* God, my *people's* God, *my* God.

- We must recognize and realize the humanity among the miraculous.

One of the incredible moments in this passage is when God tells Moses, "I will be with you." God did *not* say, "After this conversation, I'm headed back to Paradise. Let me know how this goes." Rather, He makes Himself clear, in essence saying, "I'll go with you and empower you to do what I've asked of you."

This was the beginning of a deep and intimate friendship between God and man, a pattern given for a relationship that we too can experience in our own lives. This reminds us very much of Jesus' final words after the Resurrection, before His Ascension, assigning us to a mission into which He will lead us.

And Jesus came and said to them, "All authority in heaven and on earth has been given to me. Go therefore and make disciples of all nations, baptizing them in the name of the Father and of the Son and of the Holy Spirit, teaching them to observe all that I have commanded you. And behold, I am with you always, to the end of the age." (Matthew 28:18–20)

- God clearly communicates here that He is the Connection to the past—of Abraham, Isaac, and Jacob—and also to the future, throughout *all* generations.

The Omniscient One, who sees the entire Wall of Time, is linking history to the present and the present to the future. And again, we see the consistent theme of "I am to be remembered." If there is a complete lack of evidence for these events ever happening, why would we want to remember what would be only a strange and mystical fairy tale? What good might come other than an inspirational point? Certainly not a foundation on which to build a worldview and lifestyle.

God directs Moses' brother, Aaron, to meet up with him, and the two go to the Israelite elders to report everything that God had said. Enough time had now passed that the pharaoh and the specific leaders who wanted Moses dead have died themselves. So into the palace he goes with the staff of God in his hand.

God turns His attention to Pharaoh. This is the introduction of the ten plagues.

And the Lord said to Moses, "See, I have made you like God to Pharaoh, and your brother Aaron shall be your prophet. You shall speak all that I command you, and your brother Aaron shall tell Pharaoh to let the people of Israel go out of his land. But I will harden Pharaoh's heart, and though I multiply my signs and wonders in the land of Egypt, Pharaoh will not listen to you. Then I will lay my hand on Egypt and bring my hosts, my people the children of Israel, out of the land of Egypt by great acts of judgment. The Egyptians shall know that I am the Lord, when I stretch out my hand against Egypt and bring out the people of Israel from among them." (Exodus 7:1–5)

A Little Comic Relief

Well, from archaeologists to biblical scholars, my interviews took a well-received diversion when I had the unique opportunity and privilege to speak with legendary comedian Jackie Mason. He is ranked as one of the great stand-up comics in American history and is well known for his hilarious take on Jewish life. As a young boy, he was well trained in the Torah.

As I was sitting across from him in the living room of his home, talking about Moses' encounter with God, Jackie stated, "That gives [Moses] the message that God is the universal leader and the universal God of his people, that God's word and God's deed and God's rule is the almighty power that rules this whole universe. The words 'I AM' mean that I am before and now and after and always, of all times and in all ways and in every direction. God hovers over this universe and controls the fate of every human being on this earth."

I honestly didn't expect this kind of insight from a comedian, but comedians do tend to have a unique take on life that most of us miss.

After a few minutes of silence to let that declaration sink in, Jackie continued, "They say [God] hardened Pharaoh's heart because Pharaoh believed in his own power and his own godliness. He thought that he was god. He believed in himself as the almighty power, and his own almighty power is being challenged by another Force that he didn't believe exists in those terms, that could actually overcome the level of his power. He thought that he was the ultimate power. It was like a fight that he had to win. It was like a fighter jumping into the ring with you, and you believed that you are the best fighter in the world, and somehow this guy thinks he can beat you, and you had to prove the point because nobody could ever beat you before. That it's even possible for somebody to do it. Pharaoh didn't know such a power exists. He refused to believe it."

Jackie then talked about the Egyptians' reaction to the plagues, saying, "They thought between one plague and the other that somehow it will end, that this is the last plague. They couldn't believe in the power of God to do this much damage to them and hurt them this much and create this much pain and agony and misery. They thought that His power might be limited in some way. They couldn't imagine that God had this kind of power because they didn't believe in Him in the first place."

My conversation with Jackie proved, as we stated earlier, that while young Jewish boys are taught the Books of Moses, they are also taught the *context* as well.

Purpose in the Plagues

Here is a list of the ten plagues:

1. All the waters of Egypt, starting with the Nile, turned to blood (Exodus 7:14–25).
2. Infestation of frogs out of the Nile, covered the land (Exodus 8:1–15).
3. The dust of the ground turned to swarming gnats (Exodus 8:16–19).
4. Swarms of flies covered the ground and filled the air (Exodus 8:20–32).
5. Death of all livestock (Exodus 9:1–7).
6. Soot from the kiln turned into boils on man and beast (Exodus 9:8–12).
7. Deluge of hail that killed any people or livestock not inside shelter (Exodus 9:13–35).
8. Locusts covered the land, eating all vegetation (Exodus 10:1–20).
9. Pitch darkness over the land so people could not even see one another (Exodus 10:21–29).
10. Death of the firstborn of man and cattle (Exodus 11:1–12:33).

The accompanying miracle for each of these was that the plagues only impacted the Egyptians. In these instances, the Israelites were unaffected and protected. God showed not only His curse on the Egyptians but also His favor on His people. He proved His complete control over all creation,

including the sun! This contrast between the treatment of Moses' people and Pharaoh's was not something anyone in Egypt could ignore, disregard, or explain.

As is always the case with God, nothing is random. There was a purpose in each plague and an order to the whole. In my interview with Egyptologist James Hoffmeier, he had addressed this epic battle and some of the Egyptian beliefs that explained God's choices. "In Exodus chapter 5, the God of Israel says, 'Let my people go.' Pharaoh says, 'Who is the Lord? Who is Jehovah? Who is Yahweh that I should listen to him?' And so we have setting up there this contest. Who really is the god to be obeyed? Who is the one in control of things? And in the Egyptian view, Pharaoh was the god of the Egyptian state. He was responsible for cosmic order. He was responsible for the proper flow of the Nile, the rising of the sun, the fertility of the fields, and so on. Now we have the God of Israel, the God of creation, of the Bible, who's saying, 'Wait a minute. That's not what you do. I'm the One who controls all these things.' So God begins with the Nile and ends in the ninth plague with the sun. And these two things that Pharaoh is said to control are completely *outside* of his control."

Hoffmeier summed up his thoughts, "The story of the Exodus is about the God of the Exodus. It's not about the pharaoh. The pharaoh is a minor character. It's really about God, because that's going to be the foundation for what happens next, when the Israelites go to the mountain and enter into that Covenant relationship with Him. God will look back and say, 'I am the Lord your God who brought you out of Egypt, out of the house of slavery.' That is the basis for the Covenant relationship. God rescued the Hebrews, therefore they are His people and He is their God."

The Birth of Passover

The final plague came with very special and critical instructions for God's people. This event would forever change the history of the Israelites and create a God-ordained tradition that continues to the exact detail today.

Here are God's instructions and the origin for the Jewish Passover recognition and celebration:

The Lord said to Moses and Aaron in the land of Egypt, "This month shall be for you the beginning of months. It shall be the first month of the year for you. Tell all the congregation of Israel that on the tenth day of this month every man shall take a lamb according to their fathers' houses, a lamb for a household. And if the household is too small for a lamb, then he and his nearest neighbor shall take according to the number of persons; according to what each can eat you shall make your count for the lamb. Your lamb shall be without blemish, a male a year old. You may take it from the sheep or from the goats, and you shall keep it until the fourteenth day of this month, when the whole assembly of the congregation of Israel shall kill their lambs at twilight. Then they shall take some of the blood and put it on the two doorposts and the lintel of the houses in which they eat it. They shall eat the flesh that night, roasted on the fire; with unleavened bread and bitter herbs they shall eat it. Do not eat any of it raw or boiled in water, but roasted, its head with its legs and its inner parts. And you shall let none of it remain until the morning; anything that remains until the morning you shall burn. In this manner you shall eat it: with your belt fastened, your sandals on your feet, and your staff in your hand. And you shall eat it in haste. It is the Lord's Passover. For I will pass through the land of Egypt that night, and I will strike all the firstborn in the land of Egypt, both man and beast; and on all the gods of Egypt I will execute judgments: I am the Lord. The blood shall be a sign for you, on the houses where you are. And when I see the blood, I will pass over you, and no plague will befall you to destroy you, when I strike the land of Egypt. This day shall be for you a memorial day, and you shall keep it as a feast to the Lord; throughout your generations, as a statute forever, you shall keep it as a feast." (Exodus 12:1–14)

While in Jerusalem, I wanted to hear an authentic answer regarding this event so I inquired of Rabbi David Hartman, "Can you explain why Passover is so significant to Jewish families?"

He said, "Each year we celebrate the Exodus as if we were there. We were slaves to Pharaoh in Egypt, and we dramatically celebrate the Passover Seder as if we were participants. So, there is always a renewal, always a renewed giving, and a new spirit into the Passover Exodus story. And the Exodus story was also a story of hope because in remembering the Exodus, we remember that in the dark conditions of history, God—the Lord—had, in some way made possible through Moses, our liberation. So there is always a faith that the Covenant says that God will not abandon Israel and that we are a people with whom God has a special relationship."

Of course, this rabbi believed the stories of the Torah actually occurred, but what about Jewish archaeologists who *do not* believe it really happened as the Bible depicts? Earlier in the book, I introduced Israel Finkelstein. In my interview, I asked him, "Do you believe in celebrating Passover?"

He replied with conviction, "Sure, celebrating the Passover? Definitely. I think that I make a distinction in my private life, in my life as a scholar, in my life as part of a family. I make a very clear distinction between scholarship and tradition. When I sit at a Passover meal and we read the Haggadah with the family, that evening, it's all history, from A to Z. Perfect history. Because history is not only about the time of Moses, let's say. History is also about all those many generations of my forefathers who were sitting at the same table at Passover at the same time and reciting the Haggadah. This is also history, which means that I am part of something bigger—which goes on and on for many generations, and this is important for me. So, yes, the answer is that there is a clear distinction between the two."

I continued, "What would you say to those people who are concerned with the idea that these stories didn't happen as they were written?"

Finkelstein answered firmly, "I would tell them that this is not important. Whether the stories, whether things happened exactly in that way is not important. I think that it is more important to understand the meaning of Exodus, the moral of Exodus, for our civilization, for humanity, for mankind, for understanding the biblical text and the authors. This, in my opinion, is more important."

While records confirm that Passover has a long history as a Jewish observance, many believe it is difficult to explain the origin if there was no actual event on which it is based, particularly as it is described in such vivid detail.

Jesus—Our Passover

While what I am about to share has been connected by many theologians, I feel this is yet another point to once again make the Old-Testament-to-New-Testament connection—the Exodus to the Crucifixion, the Red Sea to the Resurrection, Moses to Jesus. With God, every detail matters because it all points to our salvation.

The sacrificial lamb from which each family had to gather blood for their doorpost is a foreshadowing of the blood of the sacrificial Lamb—Jesus. The blood spread around the front door of the family home in Egypt allowed for the salvation of the firstborn in that home. The blood that Jesus shed on the cross, when allowed to spread around the doorpost of our own hearts, allows for the salvation in our own souls. The "passing over" of the death that moved through the land that night was because of the blood-marked homes. The "passing over" of eternal death occurs when the blood of Christ marks our hearts. The lamb's shed blood meant new life with a fresh start was about to come to the children of Israel. In Christ, the Lamb of God's shed blood means new life with a fresh start that comes to the now-adopted child of God.

One of the historic names for Christ is "Our Passover." Paul speaks of this in 1 Corinthians 5:7–8:

> *Cleanse out the old leaven that you may be a new lump, as you really are unleavened. For Christ, our Passover lamb, has been sacrificed. Let us therefore celebrate the festival, not with the old leaven, the leaven of malice and evil, but with the unleavened bread of sincerity and truth.*

In this book, we chose to use the English Standard Version of the Bible. Within these pages in the New Testament, there are twenty-seven references to Passover. In my interview in Bristol, England with Professor Bimson, I asked him, "Can you have a belief in the Bible if there is no historical basis for its events?"

His viewpoint was unique to what I had found thus far, particularly in comparison to Rabbi Wolpe's interview that I shared with you earlier. Bimson answered, "If you took away the historical basis, then you've really deprived it of a lot of its theological truth. So much of what the Old Testament says about the character of God and His purposes in calling Israel are intertwined with this story of this people coming out of Egypt and entering the Promised Land. So history and theology are tightly intertwined in the Bible."

At this point of my journey, I was about ten years in and began to ask myself, "Is the Bible's account true history or is it simply traditions passed down from a devoutly religious people?" After all, I have met countless people who call themselves Christians yet base most of their spiritual life on family traditions and ecclesiastical rote, rather than on their own actual experience. Their testimony speaks of a childhood belief that seems to bear little impact on their adult lives. God sounds like a Ghost of the past, not a current Reality.

So is espousing tradition enough? Can faith in God be secondhand? For me, I was beginning to see—almost on a daily basis—how crucial actual experience is to a vibrant relationship with Him. It seems this was quite important to Jesus as well.

Then Pharisees and scribes came to Jesus from Jerusalem and said, "Why do your disciples break the tradition of the elders? For they do not wash their hands when they eat." He answered them, "And why do you break the commandment of God for the sake of your tradition? For God commanded, 'Honor your father and your mother,' and, 'Whoever reviles father or mother must surely die.' But you say, 'If anyone tells his father or his mother, "What you would have gained from me is given to God," he need not honor his father.' So for the sake of your tradition you have made void the word of God. You hypocrites! Well did Isaiah prophesy of you, when he said: "'This people honors me with their lips, but their heart is far from me; in vain do they worship me, teaching as doctrines the commandments of men.'" And he called the people to him and said to them, "Hear and understand: it is not what goes into the mouth that defiles a person, but what comes out of the mouth; this defiles a person." Then the disciples came and said to him, "Do you know that the Pharisees were offended when they heard this saying?" He answered, "Every plant that my heavenly Father has not planted will be rooted up." (Matthew 15:1–13)

As we close this chapter, I want to ask you …

Is your faith based on tradition taught to you by others?

Is your belief a secondhand experience based on the faith of your grandmother, dad, or other family member?

Or is your faith based on your own journey that is current and alive with tales of your own "burning bushes" and stories of miraculous rescues from the grips of your own "pharaohs?"

I echo Paul's prayer for you …

 I do not cease to give thanks for you, remembering you in my prayers, that the God of our Lord Jesus Christ, the Father of glory, may give you the Spirit of wisdom and of revelation in the knowledge of him, having the eyes of your hearts enlightened, that you may know

*what is the hope to which he has called you, what are
the riches of his glorious inheritance in the saints, and
what is the immeasurable greatness of his power toward
us who believe, according to the working of his great
might that he worked in Christ when he raised him
from the dead and seated him at his right hand in the
heavenly places, far above all rule and authority and
power and dominion, and above every name that
is named, not only in this age but also in the one to come.*
(Ephesians 1:16–21)

Chapter 6 Discussion Questions

1. In the story of Moses' mother's plan for him as a baby, discuss the ways you can see God at work.

2. Why would God want to plant an Israelite child into Pharaoh's home?

3. Discuss the conversation between God and Moses in Exodus 3:7–8, 10–15, first from God's view and then from Moses'.

4. What are the similarities and differences between God's promise to Moses that "I will be with you" regarding Pharaoh in Exodus 3 and Jesus' promise to His followers that "I will be with you always" in Matthew 28?

5. Moses and Aaron appear to constantly trust God, but what fears and doubts might they have experienced along this journey?

6. Considering the idea that Pharaoh and his people believed he was god, talk about how each of the plagues would have dismantled his god-complex.

7. With the plagues, we see the Israelites were protected. Discuss the two-sided blessing of God when we are obedient—His favor and His protection.

8. Read Exodus 12:1–14 and discuss the historical and spiritual aspects of Passover. What can we learn and how can we be encouraged by this event?

9. Discuss Christ as our Passover—the slain Lamb in relation to the Old Testament event.

10. How can traditions support our faith? How can traditions get in the way of our faith?

Notes:

....

....

....

....

....

....

....

....

....

....

....

....

....

 CHAPTER 7

Plagues & Plunder, Relics & Reality

Faithless is he who says "farewell" when the road darkens.
— *Gimli (J. R. R. Tolkien)* [10]

For Pharaoh—whichever one in history this actually was—the epic battle between himself and some Invisible Force was nearing an end. Moses, acting as the human spokesperson for the Almighty, would now be part of an event that would forever mark humanity

Of course, this account that has passed through all of world history is deemed by some as pure imaginative fantasy to be dismissed, while others see it as simply fictional stories to hand down in tradition for principled instruction. Then a third group believes the Creator God was intervening once again in reality and history to reach and teach mankind.

At midnight the Lord struck down all the firstborn in the land of Egypt, from the firstborn of Pharaoh who sat on his throne to the firstborn of the captive who was in the dungeon, and all the firstborn of the livestock. And Pharaoh rose up in the night, he and all his servants and all the Egyptians. And there was a great cry in Egypt, for there was not a house where someone was not dead. Then he summoned Moses and Aaron by night and said,

"Up, go out from among my people, both you and the people of Israel; and go, serve the Lord, as you have said. Take your flocks and your herds, as you have said, and be gone, and bless me also!"

The Egyptians were urgent with the people to send them out of the land in haste. For they said, "We shall all be dead." So the people took their dough before it was leavened, their kneading bowls being bound up in their cloaks on their shoulders. The people of Israel had also done as Moses told them, for they had asked the Egyptians for silver and gold jewelry and for clothing. And the Lord had given the people favor in the sight of the Egyptians, so that they let them have what they asked. Thus they plundered the Egyptians. (Exodus 12:29–36)

From slavery to plunder! Such a strange turn of events. Imagine for a moment being an Egyptian and knowing that your ever-increasing suffering is coming at the hand of your leader's pride, ego, and stubbornness. In a matter of days, you've witnessed the years of oppression your people placed on an entire nation coming down upon you. The sowing has now become the reaping. Regardless of what the Egyptians believed about Pharaoh prior to the plagues, their view might have changed somewhat by the *tenth* plague.

But by the time Pharaoh relented, the nation had endured horrible suffering on so many fronts. In fact, how would Egyptian society withstand these losses?

- Agriculture and livestock
- Firstborn sons
- Gold, silver jewelry, and fine clothing
- Slave labor force
- And, in the final act, the nation's army

This culmination of God's judgment brought about another pattern of evidence, and I now needed to seek out if there was a time in Egypt's history when such economic and familial crises occurred.

Many critics and scholars alike are quick to point out there is no record of supernatural judgment and devastation in Egypt during the time of Ramesses. But might this be because they are limiting their search to the New Kingdom only?

Providential Papyrus?

I learned about the existence of a document at the Leiden Museum in Holland, known by some as the *Admonitions of an Egyptian Sage* and by others as the Ipuwer Papyrus. The relic was reportedly written by an Egyptian scribe that some believe actually offers an eyewitness account of the plagues and the resulting chaos surrounding the Exodus.

I traveled to the Netherlands to see this ancient text for myself and talk with the curator. The city of Leiden is built on a network of waterways that become a part of the life of this community. The beauty and charm of this old European setting struck me as I walked over a canal bridge to the museum.

Once inside the large black doors, I met museum curator and Egyptologist Maarten Raven in the expansive entrance. As we walked among children from a local school's field trip, I decided to break the ice by asking, "Why did you choose this occupation?"

Raven smiled and responded, "I became an Egyptologist because, as so many people at a very young age, I became fascinated by ancient Egypt, and this happened already at primary school."

I continued, "This was your childhood dream then?"

He nodded and said, "I still feel this fascination, and it's great to have been able to make my hobby into my profession."

I told him I related and knew exactly how he felt.

As Raven took me down a long hall into a room that housed large carvings of Egyptian royalty, he stopped and stated, "Because you used the name Ipuwer, I know why you have come."

A bit surprised, I asked, "Why is that?"

He responded, "Because only people who are interested in connecting this document to the biblical story use *that* name. Normally they would call it the *Admonitions*."

Respectfully, I asked, "Is that all right?"

He softened a bit. "Yes, I have no problem with you asking questions. It's fine. People can think and ask as they like."

With the camera now set up and rolling, I opened the interview. "What was the role of an Egyptian scribe?"

"If you became a scribe, that meant that you belonged to the elite, to the 1 percent of the population that could read and write, and by that faculty, you became somebody with power. You became useful to the government, to the pharaoh, and in fact you could fulfill all other professions. You could become an army officer; you could become a physician, a magician, a priest, anywhere where they needed literate people."

"How did one become a scribe in ancient Egypt?"

"Because one belonged to a family of scribes, that assured that you could get access to the proper school system and you became more and more specialized as time went on. But the whole education could take up to ten years."

Growing ever more interested, I inquired, "What was the primary language they were writing in? Was it just hieroglyphics, or were there different periods of time when that language changed?"

Raven continued, "Of course everybody knows about the Egyptian writing system, the hieroglyphs, but hieroglyphs were something from monumental art. They were carved by sculptors, whereas a scribe would make his notes on a sheet of papyrus. He needed a quick writing system, something cursive, and that was hieratic. Hieratic is just stylized hieroglyphics."

Getting more specific to my point for the trip, I then questioned, "Now I want to ask you about the Ipuwer Papyrus, or the *Admonitions of an Egyptian Sage* as you would call it, here at this museum. What is it?"

"The so-called papyrus of the *Admonitions of an Egyptian Sage* was given that name by the first editor, Sir Alan Gardiner, in 1909. He made the first scientific edition of the papyrus, which is unique. It's one of a kind. There is only one copy of this specific text, and that is here. This is the most important document in the Leiden Museum." Raven went on, "The importance of the text is that it is a book of wisdom, a political treatise, which shows what happens if order falls away and chaos comes—and we don't want that. It's a very, very vivid report, or would-be report, of what happens to Egypt when the central power falls away."

As he told me that his estimate for the date of the original composition was around 1800 BC, I asked, "Who was Ipuwer?"

"We don't know who Ipuwer was, but he was obviously somebody in a position to address his majesty, the king. At the end of the text, we suddenly read, 'These are the words that Ipuwer answered to the king.' So far his name hasn't been mentioned. But the beginning of the papyrus is lost and so is the end, so just before the end, we suddenly hear his name. Does this mean that he is, in fact, the speaker of all the preceding words?"

"What do *you* think?" I asked.

"We don't know, but this is the general interpretation by Egyptologists—that these are his words and this is the instruction of Ipuwer, who is addressing the king."

As so often I had done in my many interviews, I point-blank asked him, "Is the Exodus a historical reality?"

With a polite but quite skeptical look, Raven responded, "The story of the Exodus is described in the Old Testament. It's part of the national history of the Jewish people, or so they say. We have no independent evidence that this is a real historical event. We can believe it because we believe in the Bible?" He paused to shrug. "There are no Egyptian sources that describe it. There are no other documents. There are no archaeological sources that could prove this took place as a mass exodus."

There it was again: no proof—or refusal to be considered as proof.

As I asked Raven what he thought of his museum's prized document, now I want to ask you, to give you an opportunity to decide what you think by showing you excerpts from the document, to see what Raven and I both have seen. Here is Ipuwer's account, along with the coordinating Exodus passages, connected by event.

EVENT 1:

Exodus 4:9:

"If they will not believe even these two signs or listen to your voice, you shall take some water from the Nile and pour it on the dry ground, and the water that you shall take from the Nile will become blood on the dry ground."

Ipuwer 7:5:

"Behold, Egypt is fallen to the pouring of water. And he who poured water on the ground seizes the mighty in misery."

EVENT 2:

Exodus 7:20–21:

Moses and Aaron did as the Lord commanded. In the sight of Pharaoh and in the sight of his servants he lifted up the staff and struck the water in the Nile, and all the water in the Nile turned into blood. And the fish in the Nile died, and the Nile stank, so that the Egyptians could not drink water from the Nile. There was blood throughout all the land of Egypt.

Ipuwer 2:10:

"The River is blood. If you drink of it, you lose your humanity, and thirst for water."

EVENT 3:

Exodus 9:6, 23, 31:

And the next day the Lord did this thing. All the livestock of the Egyptians died, but not one of the livestock of the people of Israel died. … Then Moses stretched out his staff toward heaven, and the Lord sent thunder and hail, and fire ran down to the earth. And the Lord rained hail upon the land of Egypt. … (The flax and the barley were struck down, for the barley was in the ear and the flax was in bud.)

Ipuwer 6:3, 3:3, 7:13: "Gone is the barley of abundance. … Food supplies are running short. The nobles hunger and suffer. … Those who had shelter are in the dark of the storm."

EVENT 4:

Exodus 10:7, 15:

Then Pharaoh's servants said to him, "How long shall this man be a snare to us? Let the men go, that they may serve the Lord their God. Do you not yet understand that Egypt is ruined?" … They covered the face of the whole land, so that the land was darkened, and they ate all the plants in the land and all the fruit of the trees that the hail had left. Not a green thing remained, neither tree nor plant of the field, through all the land of Egypt.

Ipuwer 3:13:

"What shall we do about it? All is ruin!"

EVENT 5:

Exodus 12:29:

At midnight the Lord struck down all the firstborn in the land of Egypt, from the firstborn of Pharaoh who sat on his throne to the firstborn of the captive who was in the dungeon, and all the firstborn of the livestock.

Ipuwer 2:5, 6, 13, 4:3:

"Behold, plague sweeps the land, blood is everywhere, with no shortage of the dead. … He who buries his brother in the ground is everywhere. … Woe is me for the grief of this time."

EVENT 6:

Exodus 12:30:

And Pharaoh rose up in the night, he and all his servants and all the Egyptians. And there was a great cry in Egypt, for there was not a house where someone was not dead.

Ipuwer 3:14:

"Wailing is throughout the land, mingled with lamentations."

So, what do you think? Concoction? Coincidence? Connection? Here is Egyptologist Raven's conclusion: "All the time we have to convince ourselves that this person can't have seen all this. He imagined it, or he had received this information from other similar propagandistic literature."

I asked him, "Because it's so fantastic?"

He nodded and agreed, "Yes, it's very fantastic. But he hasn't seen it. He just imagined it."

Fascinated by the explanation of Ipuwer's imagination being the origin, I then added, "Many people see striking similarities between these stories."

Adamantly, Raven came back, "I see no connection between the papyrus of Ipuwer and the stories of the plagues of Egypt. It is in a way, in a very indirect way, an eyewitness report of a historical period. It *pretends* to be such a report, but in fact it isn't. Don't confuse this with the message of the Bible—the ten plagues. That's a quite different story. Whether this happened or not is irrelevant. It's a beautiful literary document, and again, yes, God was angry and punished the Egyptians. But this is a literary cliché that went maybe from one culture to the other. Maybe the composers of the biblical books knew about these Egyptian stories? Maybe they have been influenced? But don't forget there's a lapse of many, many centuries in between. But this is just a literary cliché."

Digging deeper, I inquired, "Could you explain what you mean?"

"These writings are rather propagandistic. They are not just very sad about what happened, but there is a lesson in this: 'Don't let this happen again.'"

"So they are warnings?" I asked.

He agreed, "They are warnings, certainly. 'Don't let this happen, ever.'"

"And that's what the *Admonitions* are?" I concluded.

"Yes. And in a way that's also why this papyrus is so important, because this was the lesson that Egyptian scribes learned at school. They were taught by copying the great literature of the past. And as in a lot of this kind of literature, 'These are our Egyptian traditions. Better stick to them.' And that's how this culture has lasted for three thousand years."

Here are the available choices for our conclusion on the Ipuwer Papyrus:

- There is no actual connection at all; they are just two similar coincidental stories in ancient texts regarding Egypt.
- These events are too outrageous to have actually happened, and a scribe let his imagination write this tale, which is now used as an allegorical warning.
- Egyptian historical documents such as this somehow influenced the writers of the early books of the Bible.
- Ipuwer left us an eyewitness account of the plagues and the Exodus from the vantage point of being within Egypt's history.

I decided to ask David Rohl about his interpretation. Once again, being well versed in all things Egypt, he offered his thoughts: "Most Egyptologists would say that this story is a didactic story. It's a story of morals, telling about how Egypt can collapse if Pharaoh isn't in control. It's a type of literature they call pessimistic literature, which we have in the ancient world, which basically says, when all collapses into chaos, it's because the king is not taking responsibility for his duties. But it's usually based on events and realities. You don't write stories like that, and didactic tales like that, in a situation where you have no real historical events to back it up. It's from experience. And why not the story of Exodus?"

The Iliad, the legendary ancient Greek poem attributed to Homer, was an account of the Trojan War. For centuries many considered the entire war and the existence of the city of Troy to be merely a poetic invention. But that all changed in 1871 when Troy was discovered!

What about the United States' national anthem "The Star Spangled Banner"? Hundreds of years from now, will historians begin to separate the song's words from the reality of the war with England and say it was just a popular poem or song with no real connection to the nation's history?

Miriam Lichtheim, author of the book *Ancient Egyptian Literature*, offered why she felt that Ipuwer could not be referring to actual events. Agreeing with other scholars such as Raven, she stated, "[T]he description of chaos in the *Admonitions* is inherently contradictory, hence historically impossible: On the one hand, the land is said to suffer from total want; on the other hand, the poor are described as having become rich, of wearing fine clothes, and generally of disposing of all that once belonged to their masters."

However, the biblical account offers explanation as to how this apparent contradiction occurred. The scene described by Ipuwer actually echoes the Scripture in an amazing way.

Exodus 12:35–36:
The people of Israel had also done as Moses told them, for they had asked the Egyptians for silver and gold jewelry and for clothing. And the Lord had given the people favor in the sight of the Egyptians, so that they let them have what they asked. Thus they plundered the Egyptians.

Ipuwer 6:3, 2:4–5, 3:2–3:
"People are stripped of clothes. ... The slave takes what he finds. ...
Behold, gold, lapis lazuli, silver and turquoise, carnelian, amethysts,
emeralds and all precious stones are strung on the necks of female slaves."

Several months after the Exodus, when the Israelites were at Mount Sinai, Exodus 28 gives instructions for the precious stones to be used in the priest's breastplate. How would Israelite slaves have quickly acquired these precious gems?

Exodus 28:17–20:
You shall set in it four rows of stones. A row of sardius, topaz, and carbuncle shall be the first row; and the second row an emerald, a sapphire, and a diamond; and the third row a jacinth, an agate, and an amethyst; and the fourth row a beryl, an onyx, and a jasper. They shall be set in gold filigree.

Imaginative tales of destruction brought to the ear of the king? For what purpose? Propaganda? Warnings?

Contradictions? Historically impossible? Or eyewitness accounts given as proof of history and reality?

In my final moments with Raven, he connected the same argument so many others had as he said, "It's out of the question that this can refer to one and the same event. Conventional chronology has it that the Exodus took place somewhere during the Ramesside Period in Egypt, maybe around 1200 BC. Whereas our papyrus, when you look at the grammar and literary figures and so forth, there's no question that it was composed in the Middle Kingdom and it is six, seven, eight hundred years earlier."

We see here another scholar's bias encroaching, this time in the form of exaggeration. Even by Raven's own dating, these are six hundred years apart, yet he reports them as being six hundred to eight hundred years apart. As we have previously discussed, most Ramesses Exodus proponents put the Exodus at about 1250 BC. And most linguists put the original composition of the Ipuwer Papyrus very late in the Middle Kingdom or around 1700 BC. That would actually place these about four hundred and fifty years apart, not as much as eight hundred. Raven is trying to make the Ipuwer-to-Exodus link sound as radical as possible.

Yet another piece of evidence—the Ipuwer Papyrus—along with most all the other evidence I had brought to the table, was actually converging in the Middle Kingdom, not at the time of Ramesses. David Rohl's challenge rang true: "Is it just another coincidence that this document was originally composed in the *only* period when Egypt's Delta was dominated by large numbers of Semites?"

Environment vs. Experience

There is one very strong human dynamic I continually witnessed in most all of my interviews: people look at evidence through their particular worldview and filters, thereby making a decision as to what they will believe.

I honestly don't think I met a single scholar, scientist, expert, or theologian whom I suspected I could change their mind or sway their thinking. I certainly never tried, because my only goal was to gather evidence. I simply asked questions and listened to their personal conclusions. But in reflecting on all those hours of interviews, I saw that people of all nationalities and origins felt very strongly, often passionately, about what they believed. While most were respectful or tolerant of opposing opinions, there was always an air of knowing they were right and the opposite thought was wrong. Such is the human nature of us all.

With seeing and hearing each person's firm grasp of the "truth," I also had to wonder how anyone ever changes their mind? The entire Exodus story centers on Pharaoh refusing to change until the pressure was so incredibly great that he finally buckled. But then, as we'll see next, he changed back and decided to renege on his agreement with Moses and God.

In the American culture, particularly over the past fifty years, we can witness the life of a teenager who believes in God, goes to church and attends their youth group, reads their Bible, goes on mission trips, and has no problem even telling someone how to become a Christian. The young adult can exude strong evidence that a long-term lifestyle is firmly implanted.

This same teen can graduate from high school, move away to college, and, somewhere inside the next two years, become so shaken and challenged about their beliefs that they all but renounce their faith. And some actually do. A mind apparently made up quickly changed. Why is this? How does this happen?

So often a young person's belief system is based on family, tradition, and social community. The answer to the question of "Why do you believe in God and the Bible?" is often met with "Well, we just do." This answer never satisfies the question, but leaves them defenseless against the coming questions they will face from all sides out in the culture. Somehow, within all the sermons, teaching, and hours spent inside church walls, *environment* never translated into *experience*. Because they are told what to believe while not understanding the context of belief in relationship with other opposing viewpoints, the teen leaves home with a wide foundation that's only a few inches thick. The tree appeared healthy, the branches looked good, and some fruit was showing, but the roots weren't very deep.

So, he or she has a few highly educated and articulate professors—much like many of the folks I interviewed—that tell them belief in God is ludicrous and ridiculous. They explain there is no real evidence for this God they were told about in bedtime fairy tales and fictional allegories. Their new friends have no interest in believing anything other than "eating and drinking, for tomorrow we die." Their questions to those in their church rarely get thoughtful answers, hence there is no spiritual water or food and the roots simply dry up. The fruit stops growing and shrivels away. The foundation begins to crack. The new environment creates a new experience, finding fault and casting doubt on the One he or she spent the past eighteen to twenty-one years believing in.

Our world today is filled with people who believed the evidence was real but later were told it was false, so, rather than dig in and spend time and energy asking questions and researching, they go with the new evidence—or lack of it—and the mind is forever changed.

There is an account in three of the four Gospels of a quite intriguing moment between Jesus and His disciples. The interaction quickly focuses in on Peter, however. Typically, we see the more important a story seems to be, the more likely it is to be repeated in more than one Gospel. When an event is recorded in three, we should look quite closely.

Now when Jesus came into the district of Caesarea Philippi, he asked his disciples, "Who do people say that the Son of Man is?" And they said, "Some say John the Baptist, others say Elijah, and others Jeremiah or one of the prophets." He said to them, "But who do you say that I am?" (Matthew 16:13–15)

At this stage of Jesus' ministry, there was a great deal of debate and conjecture as to who He actually was. He wanted to know what the disciples had heard. But as so often Jesus did, the first question wasn't really His target. He wanted to see the personal conclusion at which they were arriving. These men had been inside Jesus' public environment for a while now, but what was their personal experience with Him?

Simon Peter replied, "You are the Christ, the Son of the living God." (Matthew 16:16)

Peter had evidently made his decision and took this opportunity to boldly answer. But he hadn't made his conclusion based on hearing the many opinions and debates of the people, weighing out all his options, and then deciding. No. He had listened to the God of his ancestors. He had heard from the God of his history. Jesus, knowing Peter's heart, could see and sense his faith, his experience.

And Jesus answered him, "Blessed are you, Simon Bar-Jonah! For flesh and blood has not revealed this to you, but my Father who is in heaven." (Matthew 16:17)

Through my years of speaking with well-intentioned and highly informed experts, I saw the effects of making a decision of the mind without involving the heart. Physical evidence, archaeological digs, ancient texts, and the myriad of interpretations can only offer us options for a mental decision. At some point, I came to see that we must face the same decision Peter did in that well-recorded moment when the God of Heaven and Earth, manifest in human form, asked, "Who do you say that I am?" Ironically, Jesus' question contains the same words God told Moses, "I Am that I Am."

You can argue over the validity of artifacts. You can debate the authenticity of relics. You can come to your own conclusions on history. But you cannot dispute the reality of a changed life.

 For what will it profit a man if he gains the whole world and forfeits his soul? (Matthew 16:26)

Chapter 7 Discussion Questions

1. Of these three conclusions listed—1–Pure imaginative fantasy to be dismissed, 2–Fictional stories handed down in tradition for principled instruction, and 3–Belief in the Creator God intervening in reality and history to reach and teach mankind—discuss how these are reflected in today's culture and beliefs.

2. Read through and discuss the events of the Exodus and the Ipuwer Papyrus's corresponding writings.

3. Discuss Raven's response to the Ipuwer Papyrus. Why might someone of his position come to such a conclusion on the document's historicity?

4. Why might Raven suggest the Bible scribes could have been influenced by Egyptian scribes?

5. Discuss The Iliad and "The Star Spangled Banner" examples in relation to the Ipuwer Papyrus.

6. Why do you think it is so difficult to change someone's mind on an issue they have come to believe?

7. Why do we all tend to believe our conclusion is the most correct and best decision?

8. Discuss the Environment vs. Experience concept.

9. Why is a personal decision so important in matters of faith?

10. Discuss this statement: "You cannot dispute the reality of a changed life."

Notes:

....

....

....

....

....

....

....

....

....

....

....

....

 CHAPTER 8

Needles in Haystacks

I will not follow where the path may lead, but I will go where there is no path, and I will leave a trail.
— *Muriel Strode* [11]

Early in this journey, I befriended Rabbi Manis Friedman, who resides near me in Saint Paul. A member of Judaism's Orthodox branch, he teaches around the world. The rabbi was of great help in telling the Bible stories in our film. His strong presence made for a fascinating presentation of the Exodus.

In talking about the final plague leading to the Exodus event, Rabbi Freidman shared, "The tenth plague, the death of the firstborn, affected everybody. Even Pharaoh's firstborn died that night. And the will of the people, the Egyptians, was completely shattered. The tenth plague also broke Pharaoh's defiance of God, and he finally let Moses and the people go. In fact, out of fear the Egyptians urged the Israelites to leave, and Moses told the Israelites to ask the Egyptians for silver and gold jewelry, and for fine clothing. And the Lord gave the people favor in the sight of the Egyptians, so that they let them have what they asked. Thus, they plundered Egypt. After the final plague, Moses led them out of Egypt into the wilderness to worship God."

He Will Fight for Us

The nation of Israel was given their freedom from the bondage of slavery in Egypt. They took the blessings of great provision for their journey and began their trek to the Promised Land. At some point after the Israelites had a reasonable head start, Pharaoh began having second thoughts about losing his slave labor force and decided to recapture them. Being defeated by God and Moses was likely beginning to sting as well. So he bridled up over six hundred chariots and horsemen, taking off at breakneck speed to head Moses off. Meanwhile, the Israelites were camped out by the Red Sea (Exodus 14:5–9).

Now, imagine their shock and terror as they heard the sound of hundreds of hoof beats rumbling across the land, heading straight for them. In great fear, the people quickly turned on Moses. Suddenly with their lives threatened, they decided that returning to slavery was better than death by the sea.

And Moses said to the people, "Fear not, stand firm, and see the salvation of the Lord, which he will work for you today. For the Egyptians whom you see today, you shall never see again. The Lord will fight for you, and you have only to be silent." (Exodus 14:13–14)

To this day, there is great comfort in knowing that we need only to be quiet and follow God, and He will fight for us as we face life's overwhelming odds. This is a point we should not miss, regardless of the perceived threat level.

What happened next is typically left out of the story by most moviemakers and storytellers. An angel of God—in the form of a cloud by day and fire by night—who had been in front of Israel moved behind them, standing in between Pharaoh and Moses. A cloud of darkness was placed over Pharaoh's army, while a bright light lit up the night sky for all the Israelites. (Exodus 14:19–20).

Upon God's command, Moses then stretched out his hand over the sea, and a strong wind not only pushed back the expansive waters to divide it in two but also dried out the exposed ground. As the people stepped onto the seabed, the waters created dividing walls on each side. At some point during this final stage of the Exodus, Pharaoh realized what was happening and ordered his army to resume chase. The pillar of fire and the cloud "threw the Egyptian forces into a panic" (Exodus 14:24–25). The army, realizing God was once again coming against them as He had in Egypt with the plagues, called out to retreat. But the command came too late.

As Moses reached the other side of the sea, and while his people were still walking out from the seabed, God told Moses to stretch out his hand once again. The Red Sea began to close back up from the far side.

The waters returned and covered the chariots and the horsemen; of all the host of Pharaoh that had followed them into the sea, not one of them remained. But the people of Israel walked on dry ground through the sea, the waters being a wall to them on their right hand and on their left. Thus the Lord saved Israel that day from the hand of the Egyptians, and Israel saw the Egyptians dead on the seashore. Israel saw the great power that the Lord used against the Egyptians, so the people feared the Lord, and they believed in the Lord and in his servant Moses. (Exodus 14:28–31)

Not one of the children of Israel was lost, while not one of Pharaoh's army survived. God's chosen people were safely on the other side, pointed toward the Promised Land, their enemy now destroyed, never to threaten them again. Exodus 15 then begins with a nationwide celebration and worship service, while Moses' approval ratings soared.

On the Other Side

Earlier in this book, I shared the correlation of the lamb's blood on the Hebrew doorposts to save their firstborn to Christ's sacrificial blood placed on the "doorposts of our hearts" to save us. Here, I want to make another

Old-Testament-to-New-Testament connection, creating more foreshadowing of God's work in salvation. This reference is what happens *after* His blood saves us. He has a new place for us to go—an Exodus, if you will, through life into eternity.

Once we have accepted Christ and His blood has redeemed us, salvation becomes both an event and a life-long journey—a starting line and a race to run (Romans 6:16–19). Walking through this world for several decades between redemption and Heaven is much like walking through the parted Red Sea between Egypt and the Promised Land. We know life could close in and swallow us at any moment, bringing death, while the Enemy of our souls, the Accuser, is nipping at our heels with his only goal being to "steal, kill, and destroy" (Revelation 12:10; 1 Peter 5:8; John 10:10).

But if we keep our eyes on the Lord and follow Him, He will see us through to the other side, reserving a place for us in His Heaven (John 14:2–3; Hebrews 12:1–2). Once there, we no longer have to be concerned with the past, the "Egypt" where we were enslaved, or the threats of the Enemy, because God through Jesus Christ has taken care of death and Hell and we are now where only He resides—the other side of this life.

Then I saw a new heaven and a new earth, for the first heaven and the first earth had passed away, and the sea was no more. And I saw the holy city, new Jerusalem, coming down out of heaven from God, prepared as a bride adorned for her husband. And I heard a loud voice from the throne saying, "Behold, the dwelling place of God is with man. He will dwell with them, and they will be his people, and God himself will be with them as their God. He will wipe away every tear from their eyes, and death shall be no more, neither shall there be mourning, nor crying, nor pain anymore, for the former things have passed away." And he who was seated on the throne said, "Behold, I am making all things new." Also he said, "Write this down, for these words are trustworthy and true." And he said to me, "It is done! I am the Alpha and the Omega, the beginning and the end." (Revelation 21:1–6)

The Exodus is a grand picture of all God's adopted children walking out salvation in the world by faith, enduring the many dangers and threats, until we reach the place God has prepared for those who love Him.

For you did not receive the spirit of slavery to fall back into fear, but you have received the Spirit of adoption as sons, by whom we cry, "Abba! Father!" (Romans 8:15)

Timing is Everything

I had now seen evidence that fits every one of our first four steps on the Wall of Time—the biblical sequence of Arrival, Multiplication, Slavery, and Judgment. However, most scholars wouldn't recognize what I had found. Remember, we are dealing with two separate timelines here—biblical and Egyptian. It is up to the scholars to determine how they fit together. Could they have been looking at the wrong time for evidence of the Exodus because, in all likelihood, the event occurred centuries earlier than they assumed? And if they have been looking in the wrong time period, the evidence would not fit the Bible's story, thereby explaining their skepticism.

To clarify this concept using an example in American history, what if thousands of years from now a team of archaeologists searched for evidence of George Washington and the Revolutionary War in the 21st century? Those events, of course, happened in the 18th century and would never be found. As they discussed their research, the archaeologists could eventually conclude that the war and its great hero must only be a legend with no basis in actual history—just a myth about how a great nation began.

But then, what if somehow they discovered their assumed date for the search was wrong? This would allow them opportunity to search for patterns of evidence in other periods. When the 1700s were examined, the supporting evidence would suddenly emerge, shedding new light on the actual birth of a nation. Doubt would give way to discovery.

So, let's recap the journey up to this point in a single sentence: Ramesses is still the historical giant standing in between the evidence and the Exodus.

But by this point, I had gathered a great deal of intriguing information through various sources. Here are the primary reasons I was growing ever more doubtful that Ramesses was the pharaoh of the Exodus:

- The lack of a national collapse during his reign.
- The archaeology that showed Jericho and other Conquest cities had long been empty ruins during the time of Ramesses.
- 1 Kings 6:1 puts the date 200 years before Ramesses—480 years from the beginning of Solomon's temple back to the Exodus.
- The mention in the Bible that the pharaoh who built the city of Ramesses died before the Israelites' Exodus out of Egypt. So, according to Scripture, this would have been impossible for the pharaoh who built the city of Ramesses to still be alive at the time of the Exodus.
- Ramesses' sixty-seven-year reign, dying at the age of ninety-seven, does not fit the forty-year limit for the pharaoh of the Exodus.
- The discovery of Ramesses' well-preserved mummy, meaning he obviously did not drown and disappear into the Red Sea.

Israel Inscribed

While I was in Egypt at the same time as David Rohl, he took me to see a replica of a monument known as the Merneptah Stele. It was erected only a few years after Ramesses' death, by his thirteenth son, Merneptah, who became the next pharaoh to reign after his father. The inscriptions found there are important because they place both he and his father at a different time in history—after Israel was already a nation.

Rohl began to explain its purpose while kneeling beside the inscription-laden stone: "It's like a summary of the achievements of the dynasty, and he lists here, in a poetic form, all the different conquered nations, the nations that are at peace. But right at the bottom, you have three crucial

lines, because this is where we find a link to the Bible." He pointed to the lower portion of the monument as he sounded out the hieroglyphic syllables etched there, "Ees … ra … el."

"Israel!" I repeated, now fascinated. Here—in the middle of Egypt—was an inscription with the nation's name.

He then pointed to the hieroglyphs next to the name and continued, "After the name Israel are these two seated figures of a woman and a man, and three strokes underneath. These three strokes mean plural. So it means the people or nation of Israel." He went on to explain the pattern of the victory poem written at the bottom of the Merneptah Stele shows that Egypt considered Israel at this time to already be established as one of the great powers of the day, along with Libya (Tjehenu), the Hittite kingdom (Hatti), and Syria (Hurru).

Rohl said, "The way the pattern of the poem works tells us that Israel was a major entity at the time. So it's effectively the nation of Israel, and it's out there in the northern part of the world outside Egypt. They seem to be a political entity."

I then took my questioning to the now-familiar place. "How significant is this then to the story of the Exodus?"

Rohl stood up and answered, "Well, for me it's very important, because if we're talking about Ramesses II or Merneptah being at the time of the Exodus with Moses and Joshua, this just doesn't fit the pattern. It makes no sense at all."

Back home in Minnesota, Egyptologist Charles Aling brought to my attention a new find that connected to Rohl's inscription evidence. The professor walked me down the hall to a darkened lecture room lit only by the glow of a projector. The screen displayed a broken Egyptian artifact. Historian Clyde Billington glanced up over his reading glasses as we entered. Aling introduced us, and after some small talk, Billington turned to the image projected on the screen, stating enthusiastically, "Besides the Merneptah Stele, there's another reference to Israel called the Berlin Pedestal. In the state museum in Berlin, Germany, this is something that's just now being studied and discussed by scholars."

Billington pointed to the image and explained, "This hieroglyph—this is called an enemy name ring. You have an image of the enemy being bound, and you have a ring, and the name of the enemy within it." Each of these depicted a city or nation defeated by the pharaoh in the area of Canaan; this was the region where ancient Israel would have been located.

"So would these have been captured people?" I asked.

He replied, "Realize that pharaohs exaggerated all the time, to say the very least. He's bragging, saying, 'I've conquered these people. I control these people.'" Billington then explained that the names were grouped in the same geographical area: "This is the name Ashkelon. This is the name Canaan."

"What about the third and final inscription—the one on the end?" I asked.

"This is the one that's caused all of the excitement because, again, you have a bound enemy, so it's telling you that these people are enemies of the

Egyptians. And the name down here, while it's partially broken away, has been reconstructed, and it's the name Israel."

I asked, "So this is a relatively recent find?"

"Yes," Billington answered, "the actual article that everybody is looking at now was published in 2010, although the original work probably dates back as much as twenty years. The person who first discovered it was named Manfred Gorg, a German, and he sent a copy of it to an Israeli Egyptologist named Raphael Giveon, and Giveon actually looked at it and said it's the name Israel. Gorg eventually published and received criticism, so he got a couple of other German Egyptologists, and they published this article, arguing that this name is Israel, and I'm absolutely convinced that they're right."

I then inquired, "What is the date of this artifact?"

"Now, there are various arguments about when exactly this should be dated, but one thing is for certain: it dates a lot earlier than people anticipated. I would probably place it in the reign of Amenhotep III, somewhere around the year 1360 BC. In other words, that makes the late-date theory of the Exodus at 1260 BC an impossibility. This is one hundred years earlier."

I then had to ask, "Professor Aling, why don't other Egyptologists see this and connect that idea?"

He explained, "Well, I think many Egyptologists do see it. They just don't want to make the connection."

Aling and Billington then told me about an article they had co-authored about a little-known discovery of Egyptian hieroglyphs that also involved enemy name rings. These contained the same word that was used in the biblical account of Moses at the burning bush from Exodus 3:15—the personal name of God, Yahweh. This name is considered so sacred that most Jewish people won't even pronounce it.

Billington changed to the next slide of some ancient ruins and began, "There's a temple down in the land of what the Egyptians would have called Nubia, known today as Sudan. It's called the Temple of Soleb. It had been constructed by Pharaoh Amenhotep III, so it's conventionally dated to about 1390 BC."

I asked, "So it's before the time of Ramesses?"

"Yes, it's way before Ramesses II. And this temple has the only known mention of Yahweh in all of Egyptian hieroglyphic texts. It's on a list of places." Aling continued, "Jehovah, sometimes in English, Yahweh, is the God of the Old Testament who delivers Israel from Egypt and who was not known in Egypt at the time of the Exodus."

Amazed once again at yet another telling find, I asked, "So you're saying that at this location, there's an inscription that relates to that?"

"Yes." Aling then changed the picture on the screen to a photo from the base of one of the temple pillars and explained, "The ring is called a cartouche. But it's not for a king. In this case it's for a Bedouin, an enemy group. Just as on the Berlin Pedestal, on the base of the remains of this pillar were carved a set of enemy name rings, each depicting a different nomadic or Bedouin group."

"So what is the connection to Yahweh?" I inquired.

Aling answered, "What they normally do is say, 'the land of the Bedouin of' and then give you a place name. But right in the midst of all these comes, 'the land of the Bedouin of Yahweh.' Obviously not a place name. It's called the Shasu of Yahweh inscription. It says, 'Ta Shasu,' the land of the Shasu (the land of the Bedouin), of 'Yahweh.'"

"How big of a discovery is this?" I asked.

Aling, obviously excited, replied, "Tremendous as a mention of the God of the Bible! The only mention of Yahweh in all of Egyptian texts. One of the most astounding discoveries that's been made in recent centuries in Egypt. This is an account, a naming of Bedouin peoples who are worshipers of Yahweh."

Billington then added, "In Exodus, Moses appears before Pharaoh, tells him that Yahweh says we need to leave and go worship him, and remember what Pharaoh says, 'I've never heard of this God Yahweh!' He doesn't do that the next time, by the way, when Moses appears. Now, it's also interesting because of the way Yahweh is treated. You'll find that Egyptians have dozens of foreign gods from Nubia, from Canaan, from the Libyan area. And normally they will build temples to them, they will worship them, they will equate them sometimes with Egyptian deities. Yahweh is never used in any of those contexts, which means, I believe, that they disliked him because of the events of the plagues, and the Exodus, and the deaths of the firstborn—all those judgments that God brought down against Egypt."

This reasoning made sense to me. Considering the biblical accounts of the plagues, the Egyptians would not have wanted anything to do with the God of the Israelites—this Yahweh. I also recalled and connected this to the Ipuwer Papyrus' descriptions in the Admonitions of an Egyptian Sage. Those writings were passed on through the centuries to warn Egyptians to never again allow these foreigners to fill their land, which could also apply to dealing with their God!

So, to summarize the conclusion, I asked, "Your interpretation is that this God known as Yahweh was not liked in Egypt?"

Aling agreed, "That's right. Absolutely. Not liked and not venerated."

I turned to Professor Billington and asked, "Is this Egyptian inscription, the Shasu of Yahweh, significant for the dating of the Exodus?"

He answered, "Well, I think it's highly significant, first of all because it's so early, dating around 1390 BC. We know from the Old Testament that the name Yahweh only comes into use in the days of Moses. Yet, here you have a pharaoh who's heard of Yahweh. So obviously, then, the Exodus has to take place before this." He smiled. "In other words, the Exodus has to be before 1390 BC."

Aling quickly added, "Yes, absolutely. Long before Ramesses II lived."

Making His Mark

I hope you find it as incredible as I do that in this chapter we have connected the:

- Merneptah Stele
- Berlin Pedestal
- Shasu of Yahweh

On the final inscription, we saw the name of God substituting where normally a place name would be written. These Israelites were not identified by where they lived, but by who their God was!

Wouldn't it be amazing if history uncovered our lives one day and didn't write reports on where we lived, what we owned, what we drove, the size of our houses, or even what church we went to, but who our God was. His presence being so pervasive in our lives that the only real evidence for who we are had to be based on who Yahweh is!

Throughout history, God has not demanded huge monuments be erected to display His power. He has not required the major cities of the world to be named after His names. If you think about it, God—the Creator of the world—has made no demands at all on our lives and in our land. Jesus did not come to conquer nations but the human heart. God's only Son did not enter Earth to rule the governments but to rule our souls.

Throughout history, He is found in the details, like a small inscription on the bottom of a huge monument or a small name etched onto an ignored artifact, proclaiming I Am was indeed here.

Throughout all generations, His work will always be shown to the world:

- Not in grand schemes of governors but in the faith of His followers.
- Not in great cities but in great saints.
- Not in the attractions of this world but in the actions of His children.

 So Paul, standing in the midst of the Areopagus, said: "Men of Athens, I perceive that in every way you are very religious. For as I passed along and observed the objects of your worship, I found also an altar with this inscription: 'To the unknown god.' What therefore you worship as unknown, this I proclaim to you. The God who made the world and everything in it, being

Lord of heaven and earth, does not live in temples made by man, nor is he served by human hands, as though he needed anything, since he himself gives to all mankind life and breath and everything. And he made from one man every nation of mankind to live on all the face of the earth, having determined allotted periods and the boundaries of their dwelling place, that they should seek God, and perhaps feel their way toward him and find him. Yet he is actually not far from each one of us, for "'In him we live and move and have our being.'

(Acts 17:22–28)

Chapter 8 Discussion Questions

1. Discuss Pharaoh's decision to go after Moses, as well as what Israel may have felt seeing the Egyptian army bearing down on them.

2. Talk through the concept of "God fighting for us" from Exodus 14:14. Share any testimonies.

3. What do you think the Israelites may have felt throughout the trek through the Red Sea?

4. Discuss the analogy of our Christian lives being like that of traveling from the Red Sea to the Promised Land, as well as the connection to Revelation 21:1–6.

5. Discuss the importance and connection of the Merneptah Stele inscription.

6. Discuss the importance and connection of the Berlin Pedestal inscription.

7. Discuss the importance and connection of the Shasu of Yahweh inscription.

8. Why do you suppose the Egyptians would have identified Israel with their God when other nations were identified by their locations?

9. What are steps we could take for our history to reflect our God more than the details of our lives?

10. Discuss how Paul's speech at the Areopagus in Acts 17:22–28 connects to the three inscriptions we have discussed.

Notes:

....

....

....

....

....

....

....

....

....

....

....

....

....

 CHAPTER 9

Right Place at the Wrong Time

History is the version of past events that people have decided to agree upon.
— *Napoleon Bonaparte* [12]

My years of investigation were leading me closer and closer to this conclusion: Ramesses just does not fit the Exodus. But this outcome would also mean that the majority of the scholars and archaeologists I had interviewed from all over the world were wrong. This was going to be a tough sell. After all, I'm just a filmmaker from Minnesota.

In discussing this issue with Professor Bimson, he stated, "I think there's a deep irony here, because one of the original reasons why people focused on the 13th century BC is the reference in Exodus 1:11, to the Israelites having built for the pharaoh the cities Pithom and Ramesses. And that has led people to look at the reign of Ramesses II. So the original reason for focusing on the 13th century BC goes back to a piece of information in the Bible—which the current generation of scholars largely rejects."

I then asked, "And would you say that's the bottom line for why they don't find any evidence for the Bible?"

Bimson gave the question a cat-like grin and answered, "I would, and I find it deeply ironic. It's a date that is based on very flimsy indicators. But this is where the majority of scholars look, almost out of habit really. Earlier periods have just dropped off their radar."

> *In the four hundred and eightieth year after the people of Israel came out of the land of Egypt, in the fourth year of Solomon's reign over Israel, in the month of Ziv, which is the second month, he began to build the house of the Lord. (1 Kings 6:1)*

This single verse, noted in the last chapter, is clearly a chronological reference, a time marker in human history as we discussed in the introduction. While still getting closer and closer to matching biblical accounts, this date of around 1450 BC is still about two hundred years off from the pattern of evidence that has been found in Egypt's archaeology.

Plagues, Pits & Parchments

In visiting with David Rohl regarding this dilemma, he told me about a discovery unearthed at Avaris—the site where I had first encountered Manfred Bietak and my initial roadblock. Rohl shared, "We find an extraordinary thing happens. The archaeologists who've been digging this area suddenly find lots of pits in the ground. And in these pits are bodies that have been tossed in. They're not buried formally. They have no grave goods or anything like that. These bodies are tossed on top of each other. They're lying strewn; you have hands and legs crossing over."

"What does Professor Bietak think this was?" I asked.

Rohl continued, "He thinks it's actually some sort of plague that's happened. A dramatic event where suddenly they have to bury people very quickly because of contamination of the living population. So it's an emergency burial essentially." (These findings were at the end of a layer known as Stratum G/1 in Tell el-Dab'a, which means it equates to the late Thirteenth Dynasty near the end of the Middle Kingdom. In Bietak's thinking, these burial pits were far too early to fit into the accepted Exodus date.)

"What happened next?" I asked.

Rohl leaned forward. "All of a sudden, the site is abandoned. These Semitic people who were living there suddenly get up, they pack their bags and they leave, and the whole mound is abandoned. And it just falls to ruin." He raised his eyebrows with a slight smile and said, "Well, isn't that just like the story of Exodus?"

So, at the site of Avaris, there is evidence for all of the first five stages on the Wall of Time:

- Arrival
- Multiplication
- Slavery
- Judgment
- Exodus

One day Steve Law, a researcher and writer on our staff, came into my office and showed me a book he was reading titled *The Pyramid Builders of Ancient Egypt,* written by Rosalie David, an Egyptologist from the University of Manchester. Steve shared, "About 120 miles to the south of Avaris at a place called Kahun, Egyptologist Sir Flinders Petrie, who also found the Merneptah Stele, discovered around 1890 a walled and guarded settlement that supported a large Semitic population. They found documentation of slavery at the compound there. Like Avaris, the evidence at Kahun points to its abandonment occurring late in the Thirteenth Dynasty at the very end of Egypt's Middle Kingdom."

Steve pointed out some key quotes in David's book:

- "Seems to have been deserted by its inhabitants in such a hurry that some kind of disaster may have occurred."[13]
- "No bodies except baby burials were found." [14]
- "The [lack] of cloth is unusual—if sandals and precious needles were left behind, why not unwanted clothes?" [15]

- "Two intriguing Egyptian letters found in the area of Kahun give the impression of an angry exchange between the writers. The second ends with the words, 'May you be plague-stricken!' but then follows with a postscript, 'Come that I may see you. Behold, we are passing an evil hour.'" [16]

David Rohl told me more about this time period: "One of the great moments in Egyptian history is the collapse of their civilization. And it only happens once in one thousand years of history in Egypt. Perhaps we can link this to a very famous tradition told to us by an Egyptian priest called Manetho, who wrote a history of Egypt in the third century BC: In the reign of a king called Dudimose, one of the last kings of the Thirteenth Dynasty in his reign, he writes that 'God smote the Egyptians.' And God here is singular. You would expect to see 'and the gods smote the Egyptians,' but you don't. Then, because of this smiting, foreigners—'people of obscure race'—invade Egypt from the north. And they conquer the land—'without striking a blow' is the term used. Now why? Did something happen in the history of Egypt that opened them up to being taken over by northern armies so easily?"

Here was an independent source—outside the Bible—stating that a powerful God had "smote" Egypt, leading to an invasion by foreigners. If Egypt was devastated by the plagues and the destruction of their army, then there would have been a debilitating weakness that would allow enemies to take advantage of the situation and invade Egypt.

Wanting Rohl to be more specific, I asked, "How do *you* interpret this?"

"You look for a collapse in Egyptian civilization, and that's where you'll find Moses and the Exodus. And why don't we put those things together then? We have the story of the ten plagues, the destruction of Egypt, the collapse of Egyptian civilization, the Israelites leaving Egypt, and Egypt itself is on its knees for several hundred years. That's what we see in the archaeological evidence of this period. That to me all fits together into a single story."

I need to remind you, as I had to remind myself time and again, that Rohl is an agnostic—someone who is not sure about God and His existence—yet he still believes that the archaeological evidence supports the biblical story!

Perspective & Perception

In my discussion with Professor Bimson, he clearly stated how ironic it is that scholars will use the Exodus 1:11 reference date as fact and truth for their premise, but yet not believe the Bible's account of the Exodus. On the other side, in my interview with Egyptologist Maarten Raven for example, he looked at the evidence in his own museum and declared it could not be connected in any way to the Bible's events.

Over the last several decades, our progressive Western culture has spilled over into many parts of the world. One of the curious and unfortunate effects of our abundant intelligence, knowledge, and self-importance is treating truth like a buffet rather than a meal being served. Allow me to explain.

If you are an invited guest to a dignitary's home, as the meal is brought out, you do not refuse certain courses and receive others. You do not tell the host, "I don't care for this type of salad. Do you have something else? If not, I'll just pass on this." We wouldn't think of doing such a thing and risk offense. We gratefully acknowledge and receive whatever is placed in front of us, out of respect for the host and the setting. The meal is the meal.

But if someone invites you to a wedding, for example, where a buffet is served, you leave your table and walk up to the food area where you are allowed to choose what you want and do not take what you don't want. The meal is your choice.

The reason truth has become a relative term and a moving target in our day is because we treat it as a buffet rather than a meal. We look at an Almighty God and tell Him we will be masters of our own fate, picking and choosing what truth of His we feel best fits our lives. We have moved from awestruck to arrogant, from the heart of Moses to the mind of Pharaoh. This results in situational religion such as:

- "I know the Bible tells me not to commit adultery, but it also says God wants to give us the desires of our hearts. He wants me to be happy, doesn't He?"

- "I believe God wants me to be a generous giver, but I just cannot afford to give any of my money away. We prayed for years for these blessings, but now we have to pay for them."
- "I realize God wants me to love my neighbors, but everybody on our block is a snobby jerk. Maybe one day we'll live around some nice people and we can really minister then."

Do you see it? Our culture has a deep awareness of Judeo-Christian qualities, yet we make the decision to accept the ones we believe make our lives better, while rejecting the ones that inconvenience us or demand that we change to fit a different standard. If we aren't careful, we can criticize these archaeologists for their pick-and-choose approach but be guilty of this in our own faith. We can be judgmental about those who don't believe the Bible's accuracy while we live as though God's Word is not relevant or legitimate.

There are two very important words in life, but most especially in the Christian life. They are perspective and perception. We'll define these as:

- Perspective—the way we view something
- Perception—how we process what we see

Sin (disobedience to God) can severely skew and distort both these concepts—what and how we see in life. Sin in our lives creates doubt, fear, control, manipulation, insecurity, and the like. These most definitely negatively impact our view of any situation.

Isn't it interesting how we can be so sure that we have seen something that really isn't there at all? But equally as fascinating that we can miss something that is so obviously right in front of us?

A relationship with God through Jesus Christ provides the right perspective and perception to any and every situation we encounter, meaning God offers us His worldview if we choose to receive it. Yet He doesn't change our reality when we follow Him. We don't walk into a different physical realm. But He does change our perception and our perspective of the one in which we live. The more mature we become in our faith, the more we see life through His eyes.

Over the years as I listened to these brilliant men and women's perspectives and perceptions, it constantly challenged me to surrender my own to the truth of God's Word and to His outlook on life.

The Conquest Begins

Lastly, we reach the final step on the Wall of Time—the Conquest.

> *Then the Lord said, "I have surely seen the affliction of my people who are in Egypt and have heard their cry because of their taskmasters. I know their sufferings, and I have come down to deliver them out of the hand of the Egyptians **and to bring them up out of that land to a good and broad land, a land flowing with milk and honey." (Exodus 3:7–8)***

Once again, Rabbi Friedman had an amazing and concise way of summarizing the biblical account in storytelling form. He recounted from Egypt to the Conquest for our cameras, "The children of Israel left Egypt and traveled to Mount Sinai where they received God's law and made a Covenant to be his people. Then after forty years of wandering in the wilderness, Moses transferred his authority to Joshua and ascended the heights of Mount Nebo, where he died. The Israelites had been waiting centuries for the promise to be fulfilled. And now it was Joshua who would lead them in their Conquest of Canaan."

The land of Canaan was ruled by many independent city-states such as Hazor, Jericho, Hebron, and Arad. The history of these cities has been divided into two major time periods: the Middle Bronze Age and the Late Bronze Age. During the Middle Bronze Age, which approximately matches Egypt's Middle Kingdom, these city-states were thriving and fortified by high walls. Then a sudden destruction and burning came upon the land, leaving many of these cities in ruins and bringing in the period known as the Late Bronze Age, which matches the time of Egypt's New Kingdom.

Israeli archaeologist Norma Franklin, who we introduced in an earlier chapter, is one of the scholars who see no evidence for a biblical Conquest in the 12th or 13th century BC. Sitting with her in the hill country of Israel, I asked, "What do you think happened with the story of Joshua?"

In polite but firm words, she answered, "As an archaeologist, I hate to disappoint people, but we have no evidence for a single mass migration of people from one country, wandering over a period of forty years, and then coming into another country."

So I asked, "What is the archaeology telling you about cities being destroyed?"

"There is destruction, amazing destructions. None of them actually fits any other. The great problem is, we now know they were not destroyed all at the same time. They all happened within a hundred years but not overnight. Not what you'd expect in the Conquest. You know, Joshua didn't live that long, if he existed, okay? So we're not looking at an event of Joshua—one man coming in with the children of Israel and doing this incredible campaign. That we don't see."

Curious, I inquired, "What is your explanation of these destructions?"

Franklin shrugged and offered, "Perhaps earthquake, perhaps local bands fighting one another, local rulers who saw themselves as kings of city-states. There's nothing, there is no inscription saying, 'Joshua did this.'"

In the Bible, the Conquest story begins with Jericho ...

And Joshua the son of Nun sent two men secretly from Shittim as spies, saying, "Go, view the land, especially Jericho." (Joshua 2:1)

And Jericho's story ends here ...

So the people shouted, and the trumpets were blown. As soon as the people heard the sound of the trumpet, the people shouted a great shout, and the wall fell down flat, so that the people went up into the city, every man straight before him, and they captured the city. Then they devoted all in the city to destruction, both men and women, young and old, oxen, sheep, and donkeys, with the edge of the sword. ... And they burned the city with fire, and everything in it. Only the silver and gold, and the vessels of bronze and of iron, they put into the treasury of the house of the Lord. (Joshua 6:20–21, 24)

Major archaeological excavations at Jericho were initiated in the early 1900s by Ernst Sellin and his German team and followed by a British group headed by John Garstang in the 1930s. Both Sellin and Garstang believed they had uncovered a layer of destruction that matched the biblical story.

However, when Kathleen Kenyon from England dug at Jericho in the 1950s, she concluded there was no evidence for a destruction matching the Bible. Why? Because she dated the demise of the city much earlier—around 1580 BC. As we had mentioned prior, herein lies the origin of skepticism that began to sweep across the entire field of archaeology.

The Walls of Jericho

Now Jericho was shut up inside and outside because of the people of Israel. None went out, and none came in. ... and the wall of the city will fall down flat, and the people shall go up, everyone straight before him." (Joshua 6:1, 5)

In my interview with Bryant Wood at his home in Pennsylvania, I asked him, "What evidence do you see matching the Conquest at Jericho?"

"First of all, we're told that Jericho was fortified. It speaks of the gate when the spies went there. And we have the story of them hiding in Rahab's house, and they had shut the gate so that they couldn't leave the city. So obviously, we would expect Jericho to have a gate and a fortification system, and that's exactly what the archaeologists found, that Jericho was very heavily fortified. When the archaeologists dug the city, particularly Kathleen Kenyon when she did her work in the '50s, they discovered that the tell, which the city's built on, was surrounded by a great earthen rampart."

Excavators found that Jericho was protected by a brilliant defensive system. At its base there was a stone retaining wall more than fifteen feet high with a defensive extension wall of mudbricks rising still higher. Beyond this, there was the rampart, a steep slope covered with a slick surface of white plaster, where attackers would have been exposed to arrows and sling stones from above. At the top of this rampart was the main city wall—more than twenty-five feet high and ten feet thick—also made of mudbricks.

> *And the Lord said to Joshua, "See, I have given Jericho into your hand, with its king and mighty men of valor. You shall march around the city, all the men of war going around the city once. Thus shall you do for six days. Seven priests shall bear seven trumpets of rams' horns before the ark. On the seventh day you shall march around the city seven times, and the priests shall blow the trumpets. And when they make a long blast with the ram's horn, when you hear the sound of the trumpet, then all the people shall shout with a great shout, and the wall of the city will fall down flat, and the people shall go up, everyone straight before him." (Joshua 6:2–5)*

Wood continued, "When the city met its end, these mudbrick walls collapsed and they actually fell down to the base of the stone retaining wall. Kenyon excavated that material and other archaeologists have as well, but Kenyon describes it very clearly and in detail in her excavation report, and she says the mudbricks at the base of the retaining wall came from the city wall."

"Do you see a connection here to the Bible?" I inquired.

"Yes, we have a number of points that are verified by the archaeological findings in Jericho, and we see even in the Hebrew words that were used in the account a very precise description. For example, the word that is used to describe the falling of the walls is the Hebrew word tahteyha. Now this is always translated 'flat.' The walls fell flat. But the Hebrew word has a richer, more descriptive meaning. It actually means 'the walls fell beneath themselves.'"

In England, Professor Bimson spoke about the walls of Jericho as well. "It was very heavily fortified, probably a double fortification wall around it, certainly big enough to have made the Israelites feel there was no way to conquer this place, and yet it was destroyed. The outer mudbrick city wall was built on top of a stone revetment wall that would have supported the slope going higher up; and that wall certainly seems, judging from where the mudbricks are distributed, to have fallen outwards. Now this would have provided a very convenient ramp, actually, for any attackers to have charged up the slope and into the main part of the city."

The Fires of Jericho

Wood expanded on Kenyon's conclusion about the destruction. "For Kenyon, it had no connection with the Bible because she dated the destruction of the city to one hundred and fifty years before Joshua. Even in the Hebrew words that are used, we see evidence that this is not some account that was written hundreds of years later by somebody in the Exile Period. This was written down by somebody who actually saw it and was describing what they saw. We're told the Israelites set the city on fire. And that's exactly what we find; Jericho was massively destroyed by fire. Kenyon said it was very clear that within the city, the walls of the buildings had fallen as well. And she says that the walls fell before the fire. And so we have the sequence that we read in the Bible: first the fallen walls, and then the city being set on fire by the Israelites."

Wood continued, "Kenyon claimed that the city was destroyed around 1550 BC by the Egyptians. Well, there's absolutely no evidence that the Egyptians were ever in the Jordan Valley at this time period. But nevertheless, that's her theory and that's the dating she came up with, and her dating has been accepted by archaeologists and followed to this very day."

"Did Kenyon find anything else?" I asked.

"Kenyon found a very thick burn layer which showed that the city had been burned, so that also fits with what the Bible says happened at Jericho."

So both Wood and Bimson could see that Kenyon's report on Jericho mirrored the biblical description of the city's fall, including the fire.

The Grain of Jericho

But you, keep yourselves from the things devoted to destruction, lest when you have devoted them you take any of the devoted things and make the camp of Israel a thing for destruction and bring trouble upon it. (Joshua 6:18)

Then Wood brought up another compelling find at Jericho. "Within the city a very unique discovery was made. Both Garstang and Kenyon found in the houses that they excavated many storage jars full of grain. When the Israelites crossed the Jordan, the first thing they did was celebrate Passover. Well, when is Passover? Again, the spring of the year."

Wood explained, "That matches the biblical account because in its story the siege was only seven days. Otherwise, the people inside would have consumed a lot of that grain if it dragged out for months."

"Was this grain found all over the city?" I asked.

"Yes," he answered, "in every house that was excavated, they found jars of grain."

"Is this unique?" I inquired.

He nodded and said, "When a city was conquered, they would go in and plunder the city, including the grain because it was valuable not only for food, but you could use it for bartering. It was like money."

I then asked, "If this grain was so valuable, why do you think it was left in Jericho?"

"Well," Wood replied, "the answer is in Joshua chapter 6, where we read that God commanded the Israelites not to plunder Jericho. It was to be offered up as an offering to the Lord, the first fruits of the Promised Land."

If the Egyptians or any other army had destroyed the city as Kenyon suggested, why would they not have taken all the grain they possibly could for their own food supply?

The Rescued Prostitute, Rahab

She came up to them on the roof and said to the men, "I know that the Lord has given you the land, and that the fear of you has fallen upon us, and that all the inhabitants of the land melt away before you. For we have heard how the Lord dried up the water of the Red Sea before you when you came out of Egypt, and what you did to the two kings of the Amorites who were beyond the Jordan, to Sihon and Og, whom you devoted to destruction. And as soon as we heard it, our hearts melted, and there was no spirit left in any man because of you, for the Lord your God, he is God in the heavens above and on the earth beneath. Now then, please swear to me by the Lord that, as I have dealt kindly with you, you also will deal kindly with my father's house, and give me a sure sign that you will save alive my father and mother, my brothers and sisters, and all who belong to them, and deliver our lives from death." And the men said to her, "Our life for yours even to death! If you do not tell this business of ours, then when the Lord gives us the land we will deal kindly and faithfully with you." Then she let them down by a rope through the window, for her house was built into the city wall, so that she lived in the wall. (Joshua 2:8–15)

Word had obviously spread throughout the region about what had happened in Egypt. Here are a few important elements to note in this exchange between Joshua's spies and this prostitute:

- Rahab calls Him "the Lord," not "that god," "a god," or even "your God."
- Rahab doesn't give Moses credit for the Red Sea escape, but God.

- Rahab acknowledges Him as "God in the heavens above and on the earth beneath."

Was this woman just a shrewd and streetwise negotiator who knew how to manipulate men? Or might she have been a worshiper of Yahweh who had been placed in the horrific situation of having to support her entire family, who quite obviously lived in poverty, by the only way she knew how?

I have always been puzzled as to why, if Rahab's house was built into the city wall, she and her family could have survived when the walls fell? Our research team had purchased from a bookseller in Jerusalem the actual archaeological report that the German excavator of Jericho, Ernst Sellin, had published in 1913. This was a rare find. Sellin's work was impressive but now seemed to have been long forgotten, overshadowed by the findings of Kenyon. The book had detailed plans and photographs of the Jericho site, including a part that echoed the Rahab story in an unexpected way.

In Wood's interview, he had also talked about Rahab in detail. "The Germans [led by Sellin] found that, in this one short stretch on the north side of the city, there were houses built on the rampart between the lower city wall and the upper city wall. And some of those houses were built right up against the lower city wall. They found that the city wall did not fall in this area. So that provides an explanation for how the spies could have saved Rahab and her family. Because God brought the wall down everywhere else except where her house was, and we have archaeological evidence to back that up."

> But Rahab the prostitute and her father's household and all who belonged to her, Joshua saved alive. And she has lived in Israel to this day, because she hid the messengers whom Joshua sent to spy out Jericho. (Joshua 6:25)

The Bias Balance

I decided to ask Wood, "What if people say that you're biased?"

His answer was crystal clear: "I think everybody in the field is biased one way or another. I admit my bias. However, I cannot make up the evidence. I cannot plant it in the ground. And I have analyzed it and compared it to the Bible, and I see how it matches exactly. That's science. Look at your evidence and come to a conclusion based on the evidence."

Bryant Wood and Charles Aling believe that a case can be made for the Exodus occurring in the mid-1400s BC using the conventional timelines for Egypt and Canaan because Kenyon misdated the pottery at Jericho. However, David Rohl and John Bimson propose that Kenyon came to a wrong destruction date at Jericho because the dates assigned to the Middle Bronze Age are not correct and need adjusting. Even so, these scholars all agree that the way Jericho was destroyed matches in great detail the story of Joshua and the Israelites.

The Cities of Conquest

Joshua laid an oath on them at that time, saying, "Cursed before the Lord be the man who rises up and rebuilds this city, Jericho." (Joshua 6:26)

The archaeology shows that after the destruction, the city of Jericho was indeed abandoned for centuries.

I asked Bimson, "Are there other cities that were destroyed that make you think the Conquest actually happened?"

"Well, all together we have about thirty sites which were either destroyed or abandoned at the end of the Middle Bronze Age. I wouldn't say the Israelites attacked every one of those, because that would go way beyond what the Bible describes. But then I wouldn't expect the Bible to be telling us every detail of what was happening. I think there were lots of factors feeding into the collapse of these cities."

"And this all happened around the end of the time that archaeologists call the Middle Bronze Age?" I asked.

Bimson nodded. "We know that cities like Jericho and Hazor were major cities at that time, and in both of those cases, those cities were destroyed by fire, as the Bible describes. So if we go to this earlier date, we have a very good fit, with a whole list of sites, a good fit between the biblical narrative and the archaeological evidence."

I wanted Bimson to give his conclusion. "Do you think that there is a pattern of evidence that exists in Palestine that shows a Conquest happened?"

"When we look at the right period, I think we have enough destroyed and abandoned cities to say this fits the sequence of events the Bible is describing in the book of Joshua and the book of Judges. There's a high probability that we're looking here at Joshua's Conquest. They are correct about the 13th century. Where they go wrong is to deduce that there was never any Exodus or Conquest. I mean, if you take the Bible's own clues seriously, it puts these events about two centuries earlier."

The evidence from the earlier Middle Bronze Age is significant because it matches the Conquest story so well, whereas the archaeology from the Late Bronze Age does not. Once again, dating is the key reason why the archaeology does not match the early history recorded in the Bible. The problem is that the end of the Middle Bronze Age is currently thought to be four centuries earlier than the 13th century BC, not two centuries earlier. However, this fits the pattern of evidence I had been seeing that matched all the other steps.

According to the biblical account:

- Joshua did not destroy and burn most of the cities of Canaan. The vast majority of cities were left intact for use by the Israelites.
- The Israelites are said to have destroyed more than the three cities that are often mentioned as being burned.
- Those cities that the text designates as being defeated and destroyed do in fact show archaeological signs of the destruction of high-walled fortresses near the end of the Middle Bronze Age.

Archaeologists working in Canaan have uncovered:

- The remains of a city at Jericho with high fortification walls that fell down
- Evidence that the city was intentionally burned after the collapse

- Storage jars filled with charred grain, evidence of a short siege in springtime
- A section of houses within the wall at Jericho surprisingly preserved, fitting the story of Rahab
- The remains of major destruction and fire at Hazor from the same period
- A tablet from Hazor containing the name Jabin, the king mentioned in the Bible
- A pattern of cities mentioned in the biblical Conquest account that show archaeological evidence of high walls and destructions at the same time as Jericho and Hazor (near the end of the Middle Bronze Age)
- A Middle Bronze fortress temple at Shechem that matches the Bible's mention of the temple where Joshua and the Israelites renewed the Covenant
- Smaller, older shrines at Shechem that fit the idea of outdoor worship previously practiced by Abraham and Jacob at the site
- An ancient shrine said to be the tomb of Joseph, lying only two hundred yards from the temple
- A standing stone at Shechem that matches the story of Joshua setting up a large stone as a witness to the renewal of the Covenant

David Rohl was the first person to connect Bietak's evidence at Avaris with Joseph, and now he was making a connection between Sellin's archaeological reports and the story of Joshua and the Conquest.

Sitting across from Rohl, I felt as if I had to ask one more question. I was somewhat reluctant, because I knew it would challenge the foundations of history and Egyptology. "The events that you're suggesting in Egypt and Canaan, are they in the right sequence?"

David leaned forward and became animated, making gestures as he spoke, "The whole thing from the beginning of the sojourn in Egypt, the slavery, Moses and the Exodus, the Conquest of the Promised Land is all there in one nice neat line ... but it's way too early."

Destiny Has a Destination

In talking with Rabbi Friedman, he said the Israelites had been waiting for centuries for God's promise to Abraham to be fulfilled. In this and other Bible stories, we can see there are many promises God makes, but we must wait on His timing. These usually are not fulfilled in our preferred timeline and way. But waiting does not mean to do nothing, but rather to actively and faithfully seek God and His purposes—as we wait.

The ultimate fulfillment of Jesus' return is as certain as any of God's promises. This is exactly why we must be found faithful to rest in the grace and forgiveness that the cross of Christ has provided. We must not and cannot trust our own righteousness, church membership, social status, or the cultural lie that all paths lead to God.

The Lord is not slow to fulfill his promise as some count slowness, but is patient toward you, not wishing that any should perish, but that all should reach repentance. But the day of the Lord will come like a thief, and then the heavens will pass away with a roar, and the heavenly bodies will be burned up and dissolved, and the earth and the works that are done on it will be exposed. Since all these things are thus to be dissolved, what sort of people ought you to be in lives of holiness and godliness, waiting for and hastening the coming of the day of God, because of which the heavens will be set on fire and dissolved, and the heavenly bodies will melt as they burn! But according to his promise we are waiting for new heavens and a new earth in which righteousness dwells. Therefore, beloved, since you are waiting for these, be diligent to be found by him without spot or blemish, and at peace. (2 Peter 3:9–14)

God had promised Moses He would lead the people to the Promised Land. From the far side of the Red Sea on the other side from Egypt, God had a final destination planned for His people. This journey was not only about what He was saving them from, but also what He *was leading them to.*

"I am the Lord, your Holy One, the Creator of Israel, your King." Thus says the Lord, who makes a way in the sea, a path in the mighty waters, who brings forth chariot and horse, army and warrior, they lie down, they cannot rise, they are extinguished, quenched like a wick: "Remember not the former things, nor consider the things of old. Behold, I am doing a new thing; now it springs forth, do you not perceive it? I will make a way in the wilderness and rivers in the desert." (Isaiah 43:15–19)

We must not miss that God is constantly in the business of saving us from ourselves while leading us to Him! As a loving Father, He is constantly guiding us to a new place in new ways. He never rescues us from a crisis and then leaves us alone. He heals and helps us on to health.

So many times, we get ourselves into trouble and cry out to God to save us. Then when He does, we thank Him and go right back to our lives that will circle us back to trouble yet again. Being in a relationship with Christ doesn't ensure we will not get lost in the desert, but that when we do, He will find us and put us back on the road to the Promised Land—every time. God's goal for us is not constant rescue but abundant life!

 "For you are a people holy to the Lord your God. The Lord your God has chosen you to be a people for his treasured possession, out of all the peoples who are on the face of the earth. It was not because you were more in number than any other people that the Lord set his love on you and chose you, for you were the fewest of all peoples, but it is because the Lord loves you and is keeping the oath that he swore to your fathers, that the Lord has brought you out with a mighty hand and redeemed you from the house of slavery, from the hand of Pharaoh king of Egypt. Know therefore that the Lord your God is God, the faithful God who keeps covenant and steadfast love with those who love him and keep his commandments, to a thousand generations." (Deuteronomy 7:6–9)

Chapter 9 Discussion Questions

1. Why do you suppose one archaeologist can look at evidence and not consider the Bible at all, while another studies and makes the connection—even when neither are Christians?

2. What might be the differences in trying to fit evidence to the Bible versus realizing the Bible fits the evidence? Does the order matter? Why?

3. How might the concept of a singular, personal God be quite foreign to a culture that worships a variety of distant and uninvolved gods? Discuss.

4. Discuss the meal-versus-buffet analogy of approaching God's truth today.

5. What are some other examples, other than the three given, as to how we can pick and choose what we will believe and obey in today's culture?

6. Discuss the Perspective-and-Perception concept. How does our faith impact these two connected areas?

7. Discuss the walls, fire, and grain evidences for Jericho's Conquest.

8. Discuss the rescue of Rahab. Why did God allow her and her family's rescue?

9. How do biases affect our everyday lives? How should our faith affect our biases?

10. Share a testimony about a time when God saved you from something while clearly leading you to something else.

Notes:

 CHAPTER 10

Of History & Heaven

We thought we had the answers, it was the questions we had wrong.
— *Bono* [17]

Despite the claims of so many skeptical voices, I had discovered that there is evidence matching every major step of the Exodus story. The problem is that this powerful pattern is deemed to be in the wrong time period, about two hundred years earlier than expected, even when using the "early" Exodus date of around 1450 BC. I came up with four possible explanations as to why so much evidence could match the Bible:

1. Coincidental Pattern

Many archaeologists today agree the pattern visible in the Middle Kingdom could be a mere coincidence, because they consider only one or two isolated pieces. But most have never been made aware of or looked into the complete sequence. The strength of the six-step pattern became our team's full motivation.

2. Timeline—Bible Off/Egypt Correct

If this early pattern of evidence is not a coincidence, then there is the possibility that our understanding of the biblical date is off and Egypt's dating is correct. This allows for the Exodus to have actually happened long before 1450 BC. After looking more closely at this interpretation, however, there appeared to be too many places where the evidence didn't line up as well with all six of the steps. This also required approaching some biblical information as merely symbolic. I set this view aside as a second-tier option.

3. Acceptance of Only the First Three Steps

Some scholars accept the evidence found in the Middle Kingdom for only the first three steps—Arrival, Multiplication, Slavery. Holding to the conventional chronology for Egypt, they believe that much of the pattern found in the last three steps—Judgment, Exodus, Conquest—is not related.

4. Timeline—Bible Correct/Egypt Off

Rohl, Bimson, and others have proposed that the widely accepted timeline for ancient Egypt contains flaws, explaining why the evidence does not match up with the Bible. They believe the founders of Egyptology developed their chronology incorrectly. As a result, over the years, historians built upon this faulty framework. These scholars recommend that Egypt be reevaluated and a portion of the timeline be shifted forward—by centuries.

For a 1450 BC biblical Exodus date to fit the evidence I have profiled for all six steps of the sequence, an adjustment as described in #4 would be necessary. So the question remains: Have scholars been missing evidence for the Exodus because Egypt's timeline is faulty?

Crafting Chronology

I asked Rohl about his proposal to current historians. Wide-eyed and fully engaged, he stated, "Let's just suggest for a moment that we've got the timeline wrong, and what we should be doing is revising that timeline.

Shorten it by, say, about three centuries, something like that, and all of a sudden these things that are too early become contemporary with the events in the Old Testament. They sync up again. Everything links together."

Though excited and intrigued, my investigative nature was determined to stay objective, because this shift would resolve my original questions completely.

When I returned to Chicago for a more in-depth interview with Egyptologist James Hoffmeier, I asked him about the problems with Egypt's dating: "Could we talk about Egyptologists like David Rohl who suggests the chronology is off? Do you see any possibilities with this approach?"

Hoffmeier shook his head, answering, "I'm very much against chronological revisionism. Very good, very competent historians have been working for decades and decades on Egyptian chronology and Near-Eastern chronology. There's still more work to be done, but I don't see the possibility of moving centuries. Maybe a decade here, a decade there, but I think we're locked in by some pretty significant anchoring points."

In Israel at the University of Tel Aviv's archaeology department, Professor Finkelstein was equally opposed to changing the chronology of Egypt. He declared, "There are some people who say the Israelites are really from the Middle Bronze Age. They think a better Egyptian chronology would solve the problem. I don't think so. What's behind it is the idea, 'Well, we don't have a Conquest in the 13th century so let's look for a Conquest sometime earlier and harmonize it with the archaeology in the Bible.' I'm not into this business at all. And I think that we know enough to say that we may be wrong, ten years here, ten years there, but there's no way to shift centuries. I mean, forget it. Look, I don't need to go this direction. I think that we are on solid ground."

Along my journey, I had been warned continually by scholars close to me not to question Egypt's chronology. Yet repeatedly, I recalled Mansour Boraik's words advising me to find a pattern of evidence—no matter where it led me. Well, I *did* find a clear pattern, and I had *followed* it—straight into an archaeological roadblock. The majority of scholars, even many of those who believe in the Bible, won't allow the evidence I've seen to be connected to the Exodus. But this pattern was so strong I just couldn't let it go.

Rags and Tatters

A week before my wife and I were leaving on a trip to England, my co-worker Steve Law asked, "How close will you be to Oxford?"

"I don't know. Why?" I wondered.

He continued, "Have you heard of Sir Alan Gardiner?"

"Of course. He's one of the greatest Egyptologists of the 20th century," I responded.

Steve explained, "Well, I've been digging around and found something he wrote that I think gives another side of the story. It might help you counter the pushback you've received from scholars about Egypt's chronology."

Looking at a map of England, I saw I would only be forty minutes by train from Oxford University. The late Sir Alan Gardiner, who we mentioned in chapter 7 was the first to translate the Ipuwer Papyrus or the *Admonitions of an Egyptian Sage*, was perhaps the 20th century's greatest specialist in reading hieroglyphs. While he had made great contributions in uncovering what we know about Egypt today, he also implied that our knowledge of the ancient world was quite limited.

Once at Oxford, two librarians led me to a small archive. The room housed the original manuscripts, documents, and notebooks of some of the most renowned scholars in the world. The walls held two large portraits, one of Sir Alan Gardiner and the other of Howard Carter, who had discovered King Tut's tomb.

As I was seated, one librarian told me, "You'll need to put these on first." She handed me a pair of clean white cotton gloves, then they carefully arranged Sir Gardiner's notebooks in front of me. I was moved as I looked through his personal notes. Every time I was given the privilege of touching history, I always had such a deep sense of awe and wonder. In that moment, I felt as if I was following a trail that he had blazed long before me.

In one notebook I found a key passage just as Steve had suggested. Gardiner wrote: "It must never be forgotten that we are dealing with a civilization thousands of years old and one of which only tiny remnants have survived. What is proudly advertised as Egyptian history is merely a collection of rags and tatters." [18]

Tiny remnants? Proudly advertised? Rags and tatters? In poetic phrasing, it was as if Gardiner was prophesying how all that follow the Egyptian trail need to be careful to not assume too much on what is known, for we actually know very little.

At the mortuary temple of Ramesses II in Luxor, I asked Kent Weeks about what Gardiner had written. "Is it still true today that what we have are 'rags and tatters,' or do you think that's changed?"

Weeks responded, "No, I think that basically is true. What's interesting about the source material from ancient Egypt, though, is that those 'rags and tatters' are more numerous and of a more varied kind than almost any other civilization on the face of the Earth. The remarkable preservative nature of the Egyptian climate has ensured that we have things here that classical archaeologists in Greece or Rome or western Asiatic archaeologists could only dream of. I mean who can imagine—costume, cloth, stone, wood, papyrus, you name it—every kind of material imaginable has come down to us, not complete, but tantalizing 'rags and tatters' from practically every period over five thousand years and for practically every part of the country from the Mediterranean south to the First Cataract."

Looking through the massive columns of the temple out toward the desert hills, I agreed, "This climate in some ways is almost the perfect museum, isn't it?"

"Well, it is a perfect museum," Weeks agreed, "and it's a wonderful thing to have all of this material. But it's also extremely frustrating because it means that there's much more room for argument and doubt. I know that there is enough new material in Egypt that archaeologists will be kept busy digging for centuries. By the same token, I think there is a lot in museums that has not yet been translated, and a lot of material that needs reinterpretation.

We're certainly not going to run out of discussions, arguments, and reexamination of the facts."

Weeks went on, "There are many problems with Egyptian chronology, and I think we will all agree that those magnify the further back in time we go, but even in more recent periods, late periods of history, there are still some problems. That said, the chronology of Egypt is still a lot better founded than the chronology of most other parts of the ancient Near East, which means, when all is said and done, it's the Egyptian chronology that underpins everything else that's being done throughout the rest of the known world. It's a big responsibility, and it's one of the reasons that people look at it so closely, because in terms of reconstructing ancient history, a lot hinges on the answers."

The Domino Effect

If Egypt's historical dates needed adjusting, then Canaan would also require the same shift, because the histories of both regions are so closely connected.

In my final interview with John Bimson, I asked him about shifting Egypt's timeline. He answered, "Oh no, no, because Egyptian chronology has been assumed to be fixed now for a very long period of time. So the whole idea of taking it apart and starting again is an anathema to most Egyptologists."

I smiled, clarifying, "Because it would undo a lot of their books, wouldn't it?"

Bimson laughed. "Well, it certainly would, yes."

Considering other ancient evidence, I asked, "Is it just the Bible, or are there other problems with the current reconstruction of Egyptian history?"

Bimson answered, "There's a whole host of reasons for being skeptical about the current Egyptian chronology. Some of them have to do with Egypt itself, but a lot of them arise from outside Egypt, which a number of people are beginning to look at."

In discussing the chronology of ancient Egypt with Bimson, the Intermediate Periods—what are known as the Dark Periods where there is little information available, I asked, "Have the other civilizations around Egypt been given dark ages as well?"

Bimson nodded. "Those dark ages only exist because of the current reconstruction of the Third Intermediate Period in Egypt. It's the source of a whole host of archaeological conundrums."

"So everything is built upon itself, is that what you are saying?" I asked.

"Yes. I guess you could imagine it as a tower of blocks, and if some of those blocks at the bottom are out of position, it affects everything on top of them. The Eighteenth, Nineteenth, and Twentieth Dynasties are dated too early because the Third Intermediate Period is too long."

So I urged, "If the timeline was shifted, would that impact how people see the biblical evidence?"

Gesturing with his hands, Bimson explained, "It would open up a whole new set of possibilities for correlating biblical history with Egyptian history and also with archaeological periods. Because the archaeological periods in Palestine, in what's called the Late Bronze Age, have the dates they do because of links with Egypt. If you start moving Egyptian history, you start moving Palestine's archaeological history as well."

I concluded, "So that could bring the Conquest evidence forward in time and allow it to line up with the biblical dates."

David Rohl was animated when I also talked to him about this time shift. "It's like a domino effect," he said. "If one period on the timeline changes, then everything further back in time has to change as well. But what doesn't change, interestingly enough, is the Bible timeline, because that's not affected by it. So if you're changing the Egyptian timeline, you're moving it against the Bible timeline. So all of a sudden, things that were not in the right time period between the two—the Old Testament and the Egyptian record—are suddenly lining up in a different way. And that's the exciting bit, because that's when we suddenly start to find evidence for the biblical story."

As an agnostic, Rohl never gave me a single answer because he was defending a faith. He was simply excited about the historical evidence for what he believes to be a great document—the oldest account of history in existence, the Bible.

I asked David one final question: "What I've been looking for is a pattern of evidence. How important is the consistency of this pattern?"

Rohl raised both his hands, gesturing as he answered, "History is all about patterns of evidence. If you have one piece of evidence in isolation, it's not history. If you can string together a whole sequence of things that are happening that match a story, then you can say that story is no longer a story. It suddenly becomes history."

A Change of Heart

If we put aside all the dates and calendars, the archaeology matches the Bible every step of the way. Why does that not deserve to be taken seriously? Why won't the experts make the connection between archaeology and Scripture?

One of the great surprises to me during this investigation was that while there has been a growing intensity in attacks against the historical credibility of the Bible, many biblical scholars seem to have a much higher regard for the conventional timeline than they do for this matching pattern of evidence.

So what is the standard or foundation for our thinking—the Bible or the current popular opinion of Egypt's timeline? This was indeed a battle I was willing to fight.

This brings us full circle to those fundamental questions:
- Did God actually say …?
- Did the plagues really devastate Egypt?
- Did the Red Sea really part?

My burning question now is, "Why the reluctance to even explore this possibility when the consequences to the faith of so many are enormous?"

When I talked with leading apologist, philosopher, author, and Bible scholar Dr. Norman Gielser, he had this to say about the patterns approach:

"Patterns are really more important than dates because the argument about dates is still ongoing. So finding patterns, especially patterns that have more than one event in them, is a very important thing. I think the pattern here fits perfectly into the time period which the Old Testament gives for that event."

Another nationally esteemed Bible scholar, Dr. Walter Kaiser, added these comments concerning the dating of the Exodus: "I think there is a very high tendency here, if not a temptation, to really go against the biblical figures. Let's have a contest here in the days to follow because this is not a theoretical battle, but a real battle in which the facts will have to either support one view or the other."

For now, many who hold to the established chronology of Egyptian history will dismiss any talk of change, meaning the timelines will need to stay in their original positions on the Wall of Time. The conventional view will continue to oppose any connection between this amazing pattern of evidence and the biblical Exodus.

But there is an explanation in Scripture, as well as a pattern of evidence, even for this dissension between the knowledge of man and the reality of history. A recurring theme throughout the Bible is this very juxtaposition between God and the world. We see this diametric opposition throughout the book of John regarding Jesus. Follow this sequence, paying close attention to the word *world* and Christ's references.

He was in the world, and the world was made through him, yet the world did not know him. He came to his own, and his own people did not receive him. (John 1:10–11)

"Behold, the Lamb of God, who takes away the sin of the world!" (John 1:29)

For God did not send his Son into the world to condemn the world, but in order that the world might be saved through him. (John 3:17)

"The world cannot hate you, but it hates me because I testify about it that its works are evil." (John 7:7)

"For I did not come to judge the world but to save the world." (John 12:47)

"Peace I leave with you; my peace I give to you. Not as the world gives do I give to you." (John 14:27)

"If the world hates you, know that it has hated me before it hated you. If you were of the world, the world would love you as its own; but because you are not of the world, but I chose you out of the world, therefore the world hates you." (John 15:18–19)

"In the world you will have tribulation. But take heart; I have overcome the world." (John 16:33)

They are not of the world, just as I am not of the world. Sanctify them in the truth; your word is truth. As you sent me into the world, so I have sent them into the world. (John 17:16–18)

No wonder the collective mindset of "the world" won't fully embrace a biblical connection! There is a clear pattern of evidence that this separation has been well maintained by man throughout history.

Certainly the Gospel writer is not talking about the actual planet or even the population, but about a mindset, a secular system, an atheistic attitude, that thinks differently, acts differently, and even loves differently than God. While Jesus clearly expected His followers to not be "of the world," He made it quite clear that while He was separate, His only goal was to save.

If Jesus Himself didn't come to force God's solution upon people but to simply make His standing offer, then this places a very different motive and response on my own journey—and your journey. Following Jesus' pattern of evidence, I must follow His example and offer up only what I have learned,

not attempting to coerce anyone to comply to my viewpoint, but simply making the film and its evidence available for "those who have ears to hear and eyes to see."

Will I be able to one day change and unify the minds of scholars and scientists alike to agree and align history to the Bible? Doubtfully, no. In fact, the Bible tells me so. But might someone's mind be changed by my simply making the evidence available? Hopefully, yes.

Our job description as Christ followers is not to be world saviors but world changers. The world already has a Savior. But He invites us to present His evidence everywhere we go, anytime we can. So, really, the goal is not for us to change anyone's mind, but to allow Christ to change hearts through our lives offered as His patterns.

All this is from God, who through Christ reconciled us to himself and gave us the ministry of reconciliation; that is, in Christ God was reconciling the world to himself, not counting their trespasses against them, and entrusting to us the message of reconciliation. Therefore, we are ambassadors for Christ, God making his appeal through us. We implore you on behalf of Christ, be reconciled to God. For our sake he made him to be sin who knew no sin, so that in him we might become the righteousness of God. (2 Corinthians 5:18–21)

Blacklist & Red Carpet

We spent the majority of an entire year editing the film, working around a solid script. Our editor, Chad Greene, had skillfully organized over a thousand hours of footage (yes, one thousand!) from my many interviews to the "B roll" scenes of temples and dig sites. But the exhausting marathon was nearing an end and the film's release was imminent. The day we questioned so many times might never come was now at hand.

As we began a series of test showings to a wide variety of audiences around the country, the film was scoring very high marks across the board. Christians, Jewish people, as well as agnostics and atheists were responding positively. Surveys were coming in with ratings of "excellent," and people were recommending the film to their friends. Our goal all along was to create a work that would reach a broad audience to start a dialogue with "the world." To this very day, God has continually honored our collective goal.

In this final season preparing for the film's release, on one particular evening as I walked in the door, my wife of thirty-five plus years read me like a book, asking, "What's wrong?"

Obviously knowing my mood was evident and I could now let down, I responded, "I got a phone call from a scholar who's challenging some of the ideas in the film. He wants me to be more careful about the problem with the chronology of Egypt's timeline."

"Really? But you're done with the film. It's made. It's finished!"

"Yes, I told him that, but he believes I should add more material concerning other viewpoints."

"Well, this isn't his journey. This is your journey, and you have to go where the pattern is strongest. You have to be true to where this investigation has led you. … And how many more viewpoints can you add?"

"I know, but he thinks we're opening ourselves up to attack."

Looking me straight in the eyes, she declared, "Everyone you talk to will have a different opinion, and you are not going to be able to please everybody. You have to be true to the truth of your journey and how it's played out. You've built this material solidly so don't worry about it being attacked. Besides, what you're really doing is asking questions. Really good questions."

Jill was right. All along, for over twelve years, I had asked very important people very pointed questions. I never inserted my opinion and often never tipped my hand as to why I was even asking. Like any good documentary filmmaker or investigative journalist, I worked hard to tell the story as the story actually was. Interjecting my own faith was not the focus here, but it was what catalyzed my quest for answers.

In life, and particularly in matters of faith, for some reason people are always going to try and keep you in the safe zone, mired in mediocrity, to stay in the mold and not challenge the status quo. As a people, God created us with a love for story. Stories give us hope and our origin, heritage, and understanding about the world of the past, present, and future. Every story has a hero, and as we experience the story, we join with him or her on the journey. That's one reason why we love watching movies about every-day-people-turned-heroes but we don't necessarily like living next door to one. It makes us too uncomfortable and creates a tension that might demand a higher standard or enact a difficult change.

But God is writing your story, and it is your story and your story alone. I have mine and you have yours. No one else is responsible for holding the pen, so to speak, but you. As my wife told me, I now tell you, "You have to be true to the truth of *your* journey."

As we head into the final chapter of this book, through all this archaeological and scholarly language you have read, one thing I pray you have received from these pages is that this God who speaks through burning bushes, who parts seas and makes fortress walls fall down, also speaks to normal men and women like you and me. He gives us great missions to live out in His name. He calls us to an overcoming life, even in the face of great difficulties. He longs to walk with us on our journey, because He alone designed the road, knows the history, and holds the map for our future.

 If anyone serves me, he must follow me; and where I am, there will my servant be also. If anyone serves me, the Father will honor him. (John 12:26)

Chapter 10 Discussion Questions

1. Discuss the four possible patterns for the discrepancy between archaeological records and the Bible.

2. Why would some archaeologists be adamantly opposed to shifting Egypt's timeline while others believe this is inevitable to resolve the conflicts?

3. Discuss the concept of "rags and tatters" as it applies not only to Egyptian history but also to all world history. How might small evidences create large assumptions?

4. What are some ways we might protect our own status quo so as to not have to shift our lives too much?

5. Bimson described Egyptian history as "a tower of blocks." How have we seen that the Bible is also this way, with everything built on top of itself and interconnected?

6. Rohl stated that history is a "sequence of things happening that match a story." How does this also describe our own spiritual journey?

7. Discuss the passages from John as they relate to Jesus and His mission.

8. How do you think "the world" views us as Christians today versus the Christians of the Bible? Why?

9. Discuss 2 Corinthians 5:18–21 and our "job description" as Christ followers.

10. Discuss the statement Tim's wife made to him: "You have to be true to the truth of your journey." How does this relate to our faith in Christ?

Notes:

 CONCLUSION

Hanging Out with Hercules

Judge a man by his questions rather than by his answers.
— Voltaire [19]

Kevin Sorbo is the legendary actor who starred for many years in the hit TV series *Hercules!*. In recent years he has had lead roles in a number of faith-based films such as *God's Not Dead* and *Soul Surfer*. Kevin had agreed to provide the narration for *Patterns of Evidence*. His baritone voice is well known and forever associated in modern culture with one of the greatest mythological characters in history. He is somewhat of an anomaly, living as an outspoken Christian among the Hollywood elite.

Coincidentally, this award-winning actor grew up in the same area of Minnesota as I did. I learned that every summer Kevin returned to the area with his wife and children to visit family. So I had suggested we get together the next time he was in town. I wanted to talk with him about how my life had been impacted by the Patterns journey and what I had learned along the way. We would also film the conversation, covering several major themes.

Our meeting took an interesting twist for me. After so many years of being the interviewer, having someone fire questions at me was quite different. Especially a guy who is as big as Hercules!

Crisis of Faith—When Doubts Appear

As we were seated at a local diner, Kevin wasted no time jumping right in. "You had a crisis of faith, right? How did that affect you personally?"

"When I was in Egypt and started hearing there was no evidence for the Bible's stories, in that moment, yes, I was at a crisis of faith. I didn't tell anyone. Not a soul. I stayed quiet about what I was feeling. But, through that, I learned that a doubt can start in your mind, and over time in the silence, work its way down into your heart, and eventually poison your faith."

Kevin stated, "I think most everyone, even Christians, come upon doubts every once in a while, at some time in their life. I know I certainly have."

I added, "One of the truths I have realized over these past few years is that there's this release valve between your mind and your heart called the mouth, where you can talk to someone about how you feel, about your doubts, and this can keep you from losing faith. When we have questions, talking about those areas is important, so we can get them out before they affect the heart."

We all have those doubts and questions. No matter how strong our faith may be, these are going to come with the territory. The real question is what do we do with them. The response of too many people that reach this place is to just ignore the doubt and keep going in the same direction. Maybe they don't think there really is an answer or a resolve for their disappointments? So, quietly, they let their questions go unanswered, slowly eroding their faith. This started happening to me, and had it continued, would I have become a silent agnostic? I don't know.

What I learned is that we must be honest about our doubts. Voice them. Speak them out. That's the only way to get rid of them. For many years, the unspoken culture of the Church has tended to discourage talking about these issues. Maybe they were afraid that they didn't have the right answers. But the problem is, many young people have had questions, and when they didn't get answers from the faith community, they looked elsewhere.

The message to the Church is that when we are honest about our doubts and share openly, this doesn't drive people away, but rather actually attracts those who are looking for an authentic faith to share with other believers. We all want to be in a community that cares about us and won't condemn us for having questions.

In the story about "doubting" Thomas, when the disciples told him about the Resurrection of Jesus Christ, he replied, "Unless I see in his hands the mark of the nails, and place my finger into the mark of the nails, and place my hand into his side, I will never believe" (John 20:25). Thomas didn't trust the testimony of his friends. But what we tend to miss is how the other ten disciples didn't believe the testimony of the woman who had returned from the tomb. They thought her words sounded like nonsense (Luke 24:11). There was a lot of doubt inside Christ's own camp—and they were expressing this loudly!

Eight days later, Jesus came and stood among them, showing evidence that the One who was crucified was now raised. He said to Thomas, "Put your finger here, and see my hands; and put out your hand, and place it in my side. Do not disbelieve, but believe" (John 20:27). The point Christ was making to Thomas, and to all of mankind, was that the Resurrection was true! The event He had foretold actually happened. The Church has celebrated the truth of this historic event for over two thousand years.

The key here is that evidence and answers can bolster faith and battle doubt. Christ appearing in His resurrected body was one form of evidence. Another was His ministry of miracles and fulfilled prophecy. The disciples continued the mounting evidence with their own eyewitness testimonies. History records that ten of the eleven disciples, including Thomas, died a martyr's death, testifying of the Resurrection of Jesus Christ. All this evidence led them to a conclusion of truth worth living for—and dying for!

Bible scholar Dr. Walt Kaiser told me he had a teacher who would say, "Whenever you have a problem, put it on a back burner, turn the heat down—don't turn the heat up—or it will make a mess out of your mind. It will boil over. But keep it on simmer, keep reflecting, and keep looking. You'll be surprised how many of those pots you can take off the stove over the years as you come into more and more evidence. Because that is what life is about—expanding our understanding and involvement. And then you can put a new pot on the stove with a new problem."

I want to encourage you to prayerfully search your soul and write down your biggest fears and doubts. Then start your own journey in search of answers. Talk them over with a trusted Christian family member, friend, mentor, or minister. You will be surprised how being honest about your questions regarding life and spiritual matters will help you overcome doubts and strengthen your faith.

> *For with the heart one believes and is justified, and with the mouth one confesses and is saved. (Romans 10:10)*

Finding Purpose—God's Calling

While carving out a career in Hollywood, Kevin Sorbo has seen many different types of individuals and lifestyles, but as he stated, they all have one thing in common: "At some point in their lives, they wonder, 'Why? Why am I here?'"

"A lot of people feel like that," I replied, "'What's the purpose of my life?' That's another reason why I didn't quit. I kept thinking, 'Well, I've got this really enormous task of trying to uncover this story for my own personal interests.'"

Kevin then asked, "Why did you think this film was something that had to be created?"

"Over time, I began to realize that I was actually filming this for others to experience. I knew this was one of the things I was supposed to do with my life. I was supposed to go on this journey—and take people along to help them understand. For all of us, this is a big part of the whole Bible story—we do have things we're supposed to do! We are here for a reason, a purpose, and this was one of mine. ... And I'm not finished yet." I concluded, "If there's something you're supposed to be doing, then you need to get on with it. That's the thought that drove me and motivated me."

Earlier, in chapter 6, I told the story of how, at a crucial point in my journey, my wife, Jill, shared words of encouragement with me and also one very key Bible verse. In this final chapter, I want to revisit this for a moment and venture a bit deeper.

For we are his workmanship, created in Christ Jesus for good works, which God prepared beforehand, that we should walk in them. (Ephesians 2:10)

The meaning of the verse being that, before time began, God had planned and called us as His people to good works, was an interesting way for me to grasp what I was actually doing in my own life.

But, as we know all too well, the busyness and distractions of the world can keep us from pursuing this calling. When you take a set of keys out and shake them in front of a small child, you can instantly capture their attention. Keep shaking the keys and moving them up, down, or sideways, and the child will gleefully follow both the sight and sound. For adults, those "dangling keys" can take many different forms. We long to fill our lives with the sights and sounds of entertainment, with shiny things. After all, after working so hard week in and week out, we deserve it, right? Fighting to not be completely absorbed in this American amusement addiction is so difficult.

Eventually for me, far into my adult life, I came to a place where I had to grow up. Sure, physically I had reached my maximum long ago, but mentally, emotionally, and spiritually, I began to realize if I was going to go on this journey with the Lord, I had to pull away from the distractions of life. I had to take my eyes off the "dangling keys" of the world's shiny things. Psalm 119:37 states, "Turn my eyes from looking at worthless things; and give me life in your ways." The way to stop looking at the keys is to realize they are simply "worthless things." The way to experience abundant life is to look at "His ways." Before I could fully see what God had for me, I had to "turn my eyes" from what the world had.

Are there any "dangling keys" distracting you from your calling?

Don't be afraid to turn off the media and embrace the silence in your life. See it as a time to spend with the Creator of Heaven and Earth as He reveals Himself to you and the work He has prepared for you before the beginning of time.

"Be still, and know that I am God." (Psalm 46:10)

When we live self-centered and self-focused lives, purpose becomes all about us. We want to find our calling to satisfy ourselves. But as followers of Christ, our purpose changes to the pursuit of His life in our lives. This happens when we submit to His will. The transformation changes us into a new person, placing God first and others second. We feel the most alive when we are impacting and serving others in the good works God has for us. Funny how our calling from God satisfies us the most when our work ends up being about Him and other people.

"'And you shall love the Lord your God with all your heart and with all your soul and with all your mind and with all your strength.' The second is this: 'You shall love your neighbor as yourself.' There is no other commandment greater than these." (Mark 12:30–31)

Applying Patterns—Pursuing Perseverance

Back to my conversation with Kevin, he began to dig deeper: "So, how can the concept of patterns be applied to our everyday lives?"

I answered, "What a great question. According to the Bible, there's a pattern where God communicates something to a person, and then he or she has a decision to make in response to Him, namely, 'Am I going to do this or not?' There are patterns in everyone's life. In my journey, there were seasons when I didn't have any answers to some big questions, but over time, slowly, solutions and direction came and I would move forward."

Kevin, knowing well the difficulty of my journey, inquired, "You worked on this for twelve years … twelve years. … How did perseverance, to use a biblical term, come into play?"

Gathering my thoughts, I answered, "If anyone would have told me back at the beginning that I would be going on a twelve-year journey, I would have just said, 'No, that is not possible.' If anyone had said, 'You're going to go to Egypt after 9/11,' or 'You're going to go there during their revolution,' or 'You're going to go to Israel to interview President Shimon Peres and Prime Minister Benjamin Netanyahu,' I would have said, 'You are crazy!' That would have all been so intimidating."

I went on, "I was constantly dealing with the question, 'Are the stories in the Bible truly history?' Running parallel to that, I then also had to deal with, 'Am I going to quit?' There were times when we didn't have any money. We didn't know what we were going to do. I had to constantly decide to not quit. Even if there was nothing else left, I had to solve this question. Perseverance became very real and very personal to me—to our entire team."

I concluded, "But I think that's the way it is for most all of us. Everyone has choices. If you look at your life and ask, 'What is the pattern of my life? What can I see?' Then the next question is, 'Where is God in my pattern? Is God in my life? How have I responded to Him?' And these responses do tend to form a sort of blueprint, a pattern. If we are faithful in the little things, this tends to lead us to be faithful in the big things" (Luke 16:10).

The point of all perseverance is to reach the end goal. The problem is that while we are persevering, we are not there yet! Am I glad I stayed the course and finished the film? Absolutely. But were there days I wanted to just hide, go camping far away, and sit in the quiet of a dark night, watching a roaring fire burn down to embers? Absolutely. But the end result made all the work and risk worth every single moment of the journey.

Are you in the midst of a trying time right now? Are you praying for strength to see a very hard ordeal through? Struggling in a relationship or career path? I pray perseverance is one of the underlying subplots you have discovered in reading this book. I also hope you can be encouraged and refreshed to keep going or get back on the road toward your goal. There is a great word I heard that might be a better 21st-century concept than perseverance—sticktoitiveness. In short, do not quit! The end will be worth the journey.

We are, as they say, creatures of habit with routines and patterns—good and bad, healthy and harmful. Some we know well and some we never see. The key to growth and change on every level is to never stop seeking God.

And I tell you, ask, and it will be given to you; seek, and you will find; knock, and it will be opened to you. (Luke 11:9)

But the one who looks into the perfect law, the law of liberty, and perseveres, being no hearer who forgets but a doer who acts, he will be blessed in his doing. (James 1:25)

The Lord is a stronghold for the oppressed, a stronghold in times of trouble. And those who know your name put their trust in you, for you, O Lord, have not forsaken those who seek you. (Psalm 9:9–10)

Combining Faith and Reason—Becoming a Thinker

Kevin then sat back in his chair and shared, "For seven years I played Hercules, which was obviously a character from mythology. But he came from people trying to figure out why the sun is in the sky, why the seasons change, why we have tornadoes, earthquakes, and other natural occurrences. So they created gods that they believed in, that they could say were causing these things to happen. So people then compare that, saying the God of the Bible is just a myth too."

I jumped in, "Great point. So what is the difference in this God of the Old Testament? This particular God these Jewish people, these Israelites, worshiped, that met Moses at the burning bush and talked to him? This was what intrigued me. As I thought further, I could see this was the big question. 'Was this a myth or actual history?' At the time I was first challenged with this question in my life, I was unprepared to give a defensible answer to others or even myself."

I continued, "I realized that, previously, my personal faith didn't actually have that strong of a foundation. Even as an adult, I was just listening to what I was told. But if you go out and start to really own what you believe, this changes everything. I had to work at that for twelve years. Today, I am much more confident in what I believe, because the Bible says there's a history there—and now I know there actually is! And once I went out and searched, I found pattern after pattern of evidence that matched all these different events. This then gave me much more confidence in the entire story—the Old and New Testaments."

Kevin commented, "Well, the sad thing today is when so many of us watch the news, read something on the Internet or in the paper, we just believe it. But then you think, 'You know what? Just because it's there doesn't mean it's fact.' It's just somebody's point of view. We have to challenge what we're hearing and not just say, 'Okay, I'll take it as the truth.'"

I interjected, "Yes, it's almost as if people are saying, 'Could you please tell me what to think, because I'm too busy entertaining myself.' And that's so dangerous! It would have been easy for me to just say, 'Wait a minute. These are the experts. They should know.' But I think that if you're a person of faith, you need to actually also be a thinking person. Be a thinker. You need to basically challenge the way things are presented. I don't mean rebelling, but rather deciding to not just blindly accept any idea. I named our company Thinking Man Films for exactly that reason. That's my challenge for all of us to ask: 'Do I know what I believe?' and 'Why do I believe this?'"

Kevin encouraged, "Well, seeing Patterns of Evidence, it's certainly made me want to question things more and get more educated about the Bible. So, speaking personally, you've put me on a better path. There's no question about it."

Then Kevin asked me about the perceived tension between faith and reason, which points to a problem that has plagued the Christian culture for quite a long time. He closed with, "You have evidence, you have reasons; you have facts versus faith. Do they really oppose each other? What do you do when you deal with that situation?"

Passionate about this topic, I replied, "There are people of faith that have pushed reason away. They feel that it's threatening."

Kevin inserted, "Because you think if you just have faith, that's enough, right?"

"Yes, they feel as if it's not having faith to look for evidence. In other words, they just believe 'because.' The Bible gives reasons to believe, and, when Jesus was walking this Earth, He gave reasons to believe in who He was. And those reasons were so compelling that people were willing to die for them. So many of us, including myself, haven't been connected to the reality of the Bible's truthfulness and the evidence supporting that! And that has weakened our faith. Believing just because we believe sets the Bible and our faith on the same footing as the rest of the ideologies of the world. People believe in all sorts of things without good reason. But the tragedy is that we as Christians have given this ground away. We have a historical foundation for these truths that the other ideologies and religions do not."

Kevin added, "What you've done is bring in the science element—with proof."

"I tried to look at the Bible as objectively as I could. Matthew 22:37 states we're supposed to love God with our hearts, souls, and minds. What that means is there's not a disconnect between these three aspects; there's not supposed to be some kind of, 'I'm only going to use my faith; I'm not going to use my intellect.' I started to see that there were many passages that talked about our minds. The Bible doesn't separate the mind from the heart. They work together; they're not competing with each other. When they mesh together, then you feel you don't have this dissonance in your life."

I went on, "Faith and reason allow you to be a thinker, to basically consider these challenging questions and then own the answers. They're out there. If people just took the time, they could solve some of the big questions in their own lives, just as I have."

Here is one of the most important revelations I came to understand: We have a historical faith built on the reality and revelation of God acting in history. He hasn't asked us to take a leap in the dark to express faith. This is what separates us from all other belief systems. And evidence has been given to us to believe this testimony. This is not to say that evidence alone can bring people to faith in God.

For what can be known about God is plain to them, because God has shown it to them. For his invisible attributes, namely, his eternal power and divine nature, have been clearly perceived, ever since the creation of the world, in the things that have been made. So they are without excuse. For although they knew God, they did not honor him as God or give thanks to him, but they became futile in their thinking, and their foolish hearts were darkened. (Romans 1:19–21)

Faith is the work of the Spirit who changes our hearts. This allows us to submit to the truth to which the evidence points. However, God has provided us with abundant proof. He does use this testimony to bring people to faith and encourage people to grow in boldness in their own beliefs.

I started this journey as an adventure, because I heard there was evidence for the Exodus. Then my faith was rocked when the experts told me there really was none. Again, did I just believe "because"? Well, that's what some people promote. They say I shouldn't have gone looking for answers; I should have just believed. But if you have no reasons, then your faith is no different than all the other philosophies and religions that have no actual foundation. As the Apostle Paul said, "If Christ has not been raised, then our preaching is in vain and your faith is in vain" (1 Corinthians 15:14). So don't give up the historical legacy of our faith, the very foundation for our answers.

If we do not love the Lord with all our minds and our belief is built on "just because," then, as our children get older, they will eventually see there is no intellectual basis for the faith. So they may choose to pick some baseless philosophy or ideology from the culture's bountiful buffet that suits their appetite better. This is the fallen nature of mankind.

But the reality is there are answers and we shouldn't be afraid to search them out. God has promised that you will find them if you seek them.

When I interviewed Dr. Greg Thornberry, President of King's College in New York City, he had this to say, "If we truly believe there is an intelligent God who speaks in sentences and paragraphs to His people through His Word—the Bible—and gloriously through the created order, and if we really believe He is who He says He is—an omnipotent, omniscient God—then He can take any question that we have. We don't need to run away from our doubts, but run to them. As a matter of fact, that is the singular genius of Christianity, to invite those very questions. This is exactly what Jesus did after the Resurrection. He invited questions. He held His hands out to Thomas and initiated investigation. This has always been the spirit of Christianity and is the testimony of the giants who lead in the history of the faith."

Dr. Thornberry continued, "Look at Saint Augustine, for example. He began in doubt, not believing the faith of his mother, Monica, who was a Christian. He spent years searching, studying all kinds of worldly philosophies. As a result, his life spiraled downward in debauchery. Eventually, through asking hard questions of the Bible and about himself, he came back to faith. His faith. Another preeminent example of this is C. S. Lewis, who came to Oxford University, talking to people such as J. R. R. Tolkien as an atheist, a skeptic. And it was through his questions about, 'Well, don't all these mythologies all just sound like the Bible? There's evidence in the ancient Greco-Roman world of stories of gods dying and rising again. Isn't Christianity just another one of those?' Tolkien's response to Lewis was, 'Exactly. They're all pointing towards an uber myth, a myth that ties them all together. And in the case of Christianity, what if it's the myth that actually came true?'"

What an amazing, thinking man's answer!

Dr. Thornberry concluded, "So it was through asking tough questions that Lewis came to faith—hard-won faith. After that process, he felt as though there was nowhere else to go except to believe. This is certainly not everyone's experience. Some people believe in God very easily. But there's an increasing number of people, including many of the students I know, for whom coming to faith is something that takes place over a very long time and only after all their questions have been answered. Then, typically, there are always just more questions. Yet Christianity has always invited this journey through faith from its origin, and there's no reason to change now."

"For everyone who asks receives, and the one who seeks finds, and to the one who knocks it will be opened. What father among you, if his son asks for a fish, will instead of a fish give him a serpent; or if he asks for an egg, will give him a scorpion? If you then, who are evil, know how to give good

gifts to your children, how much more will the heavenly Father give the Holy Spirit to those who ask him!" (Luke 11:10–13)

Deep in your heart, do you want to be known as a mature and wise Christ follower? Then slow down. Dig in. Dive deep. Widen your search. Concepts like faith, intellect, reason, and depth simply take effort and intentionality to produce eternal results. Disciples of Jesus aren't made in months but years. Integrity isn't a crash-course but a long haul. Maturity in Christ isn't a sprint but a marathon.

But in your hearts honor Christ the Lord as holy, always being prepared to make a defense to anyone who asks you for a reason for the hope that is in you; yet do it with gentleness and respect. (1 Peter 3:15)

I have come to see that faith is largely a future-oriented affair. As my mother read the Bible to us as children, she trusted that because God was faithful in the past, He would be faithful to her family in the present and into the future. So it is for me. And you. We can trust God and His promises even if we don't have all the answers!

While it's great to ask questions, I can tell you from experience that the real adventure begins when you start to search for the answers.

 Now faith is the substance of things hoped for, the evidence of things not seen.

(Hebrews 11:1 KJV)

Conclusion Discussion Questions

1. How does our response to God, and ultimate obedience to Him, determine our patterns in life?

2. Share any testimonies of times you persevered through difficulty. Share what you witnessed God do in your life.

3. What doubts do you find yourself having today? How can asking questions and not keeping silent help the problem? Discuss.

4. What is the difference in making purpose about us versus about God?

5. In what ways can we love the Lord with all our hearts, souls, and minds?

6. When you were at your peak of having a proactive faith, what elements were strong in your life? What got you there?

7. What "dangling keys" tend to distract you from pursuing your calling?

8. How do faith and reason work together?

9. How can you be more discerning in your thinking? How can this protect and encourage your faith?

10. What "good works" has God placed on your own heart that you know your life needs to be about?

Notes:

....

....

....

....

....

....

....

....

....

....

....

....

End Notes

1   Eugene Peterson, *Eat This Book* (Grand Rapids, MI/Cambridge, U.K.: William B. Eerdmans Publishing, 2006), 44.

2   "History." *Merriam-Webster.com.* Merriam-Webster, n.d. Web. 25 Oct. 2016.

3   Tim Keller, *The Reason for God: Belief in an Age of Skepticism* (New York, NY: Penguin Group, 2008), 202.

4   Doug Dickerson, *It Only Takes a Minute: Daily Inspiration for Leaders on the Move* (Melbourne, FL: Motivational Press, 2015), Sept. 4.

5   Eugene Peterson, *A Long Obedience in the Same Direction: Discipleship in an Instant Society* (Downer's Grove, IL: InterVarsity Press, 1980, 2000), 17.

6   Anthony Sadler, Alek Skarlatos, Spencer Stone, Jeffrey Stern, *The 15:17 to Paris: The True Story of a Terrorist, a Train, and Three American Heroes* (New York, NY: PublicAffairs, 2016), Introduction.

7   "Luck." Merriam-Webster.com. Merriam-Webster, n.d. Web. 26 Oct. 2016.

8   Debbie McDaniel, "40 Powerful Quotes from Corrie ten Boom," May 21, 2015, Crosswalk, http://www.crosswalk.com/faith/women/40-powerful-quotes-from-corrie-ten-boom.html.

9   *Patterns of Evidence.* Tim Mahoney. Benjamin Netanyahu. Thinking Man's Films, 2014.

10 J.R.R. Tolkien, *The Fellowship of the Rings Book III: The Ring Goes South* (Boston, MA: Houghton Mifflin Harcourt, 1987)

11 Paul Carus, *The Open Court, Volume 17,* (London: The Open Court Publishing Company, 1903), 505.

12   David H. Thicle, *What Wondrous Love!*, (Fort Oglethorpe, GA: Teach Services Publishing, 2014), 22.

13   A. R. David, *The Pyramid Builders of Ancient Egypt* (London: Routledge, 1986, 1996), 246.

14   *Ibid.*

15   *Ibid.*

16   *Ibid.* 121.

17   Tom Hughes, *Curious: The Unexpected Power of a Question-Led Life*, (Colorado Springs, CO: Navpress, 2015), Part 2, Ch. 6, 1.

18   John Ashton & David Down, *Unwrapping the Pharaohs: How Egyptian Archaeology Confirms the Biblical Timeline,* (Green Forest, AR: Master Books, 2006), 77.

19   Richard Zera, *Business Wit & Wisdom,* (Washington, D.C.: Beard Books, 2005), 224.

Photo Credits

Page 120   (Plagues of Egypt) 1886 English Bible, public domain

Page 132   (The Egyptians Urge Moses to Depart), Artist Gustave Dore,
            public domain

Page 144   (Apostle Peter), 1895 German Bible, public domain

Page 154   (Merneptah Stele replica), © Copyright 2012 Patterns of
            Evidence, Photographer, Rami Romany

Page 156   (Berlin Pedestal), © Copyright Peter van der Veen, used
            with permission

Page 166   (Archeologist Manfred Bietak), © Copyright 2002 Patterns
            of Evidence, Photographer Rick Garside

Page 188   (Tim Mahoney /David Rohl), © Copyright 2012 Patterns
            of Evidence, Photographer, Ramy Romany

Page 191   (Egyptian Wall Inscriptions), The Complete Encyclopedia of
            Illustration, royalty free

Page 198   (Jesus Healing the Sick), Artist Gustave Dore, public domain

Page 207   (Apostle Thomas), 1895 German Bible, public domain

Biographies

Timothy Mahoney is an author, filmmaker, and the founder of Thinking Man Films, an international production company located in Minneapolis, MN. Tim was raised hearing that the stories in the Bible were true, but as he got older he was challenged to lose those beliefs. Tim has extensively traveled to the lands of the Bible searching for evidence of these ancient stories. The first twelve years of the investigation resulting in the feature documentary *Patterns of Evidence: The Exodus*. This award-winning film and its companion book, *Patterns of Evidence: A Filmmakers Journey* challenged the traditional views of biblical criticism, demonstrating archaeological evidence that matched the Bible's narrative. The balanced approach allowed audiences to decide for themselves whether the Exodus was truth or myth. Tim Mahoney is a native of Minnesota and an avid outdoorsman. He and his wife, Jill, have been married for 35 years. They have four married children and six grandchildren.

Robert Noland has authored 75+ titles spanning across children, youth, and adult audiences over the past 25 years. Since 2011, he has been an author, writer, editor, and "book doctor" for Christian publishers, ministries, and faith-based organizations. Robert operates his own ministry, 517 Resources, Inc, producing what he calls "practical application of Biblical truth." He lives in Franklin, Tennessee with his wife of 30+ years and has two adult sons. Visit his web site at robertnoland.com.

Steve Law studied history and philosophy before getting a degree in video production. He spent over 7 years as researcher and co-writer for *Patterns of Evidence: The Exodus*. He enjoys applying systematic and logical thinking to the issues of history's mysteries. In the last several years Steve has been giving presentations regarding the approach of patterns in searching for biblical events. In his younger days, he competed in and coached endurance sports. He lives near Minneapolis with his wife Heidi and their 5 children.